A THRIVING MODERNISM

A THRIVING MODERNISM

The Houses of Wendell Lovett and Arne Bystrom

Grant Hildebrand   T. William Booth

University of Washington Press
Seattle & London

A *Thriving Modernism* has been generously supported by the University of Washington Architecture Publications Fund.

Its publication is also made possible in part by
Anne Lennartz
William Neukom
Jeffrey Karl Ochsner and Sandra Lynn Perkins
Victoria Reed
and two anonymous donors

University of Washington Press
PO Box 50096, Seattle, WA 98145
www.washington.edu/uwpress

Library of Congress Cataloging-in-Publication Data

Hildebrand, Grant, 1934-
A thriving modernism : the houses of Wendell Lovett and Arne Bystrom / Grant Hildebrand, T. William Booth.
p. cm.
Includes index.
ISBN 0-295-98433-3 (hardback : alk. paper)
1. Lovett, Wendell. 2. Bystrom, Arne. 3. Architecture, Domestic—Northwest, Pacific. 4. Modern movement (Architecture)—Northwest, Pacific. 5. Architecture, Modern—20th century. I. Booth, T. William. II. Title.
NA737.L684H54   2004
728'.37'0979509045—dc22   2004006328

The paper used in this publication meets the minimum requirements of American National Standard for Information Sciences—Permanence of Paper for Printed Library Materials, ANSI Z39.48-1984.

Front matter illustrations: *p. ii*, the Cutler-Girdler House; *p. iii*, the Dennis House; *p. iv*, Villa Simonyi, the swimming pool; *p. viii*, the Dennis House, the guest bedroom
Back matter illustrations: *p. 166*, the Crane Island Retreat; *p. 167*, the Raft River Retreat

For Eileen and Valerie, Ashley and Carl, Corrie and Clare

Contents

Foreword: The Roots of Seattle's Modernism, by Steven Holl .... *xi*

Preface .... *xv*

1   A Prologue 3

2   Wendell Lovett's Formative Years 9

3   The Crane Island Retreat 27

4   Lovett's Mature Career 33

5   Arne Bystrom's Formative Years 51

6   The Raft River Retreat 63

7   Bystrom's Mature Career 71

8   Wendell Lovett: The Villa Simonyi 89

9   Arne Bystrom: The Dennis House 109

10   A Perspective 129

Appendix: Chronological Biographies of Wendell Lovett and
Arne Bystrom, including Curricula Vitae and Complete Works 133

Notes 155

Index 163

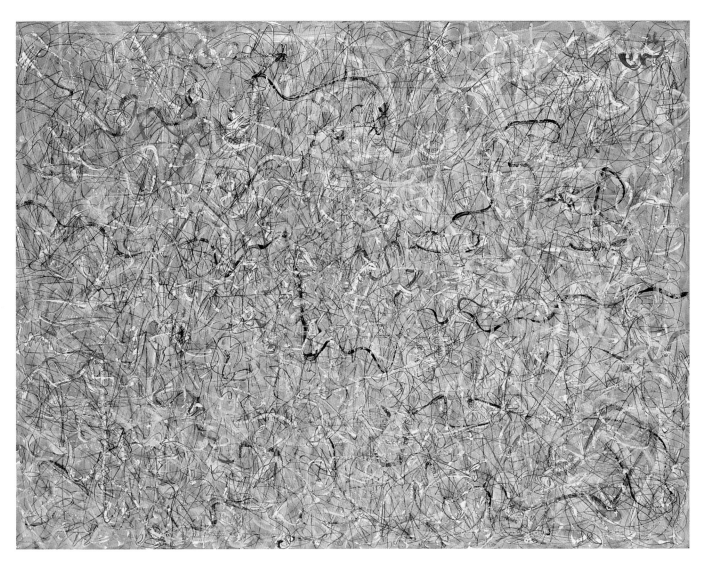

Mark Tobey,
Serpentine, *1955.*
(Courtesy of the
Seattle Art Museum,
Seattle Art Museum
Silver Anniversary
Fund. Photo by Paul
Macapia)

Foreword
The Roots of Seattle's Modernism
by Steven Holl

Seattle was nonexistent in 1851—the year Joseph Paxton's amazing Crystal Palace was erected in London. Five years later, when America's first modernist architect, Louis Sullivan, was born, Seattle's workers had begun logging, harvesting, and milling the region's giant Douglas fir and cedar for buildings being constructed in San Francisco.

With its vast, steel-blue waters of Puget Sound flanked by snow-topped mountains—the Olympic Range on one horizon, the Cascade Range on the other, with Mount Rainier presiding like Mount Fuji on the south—Seattle was a unique and celebrated landscape from its beginning. The modest cedar plank longhouses of Native tribes, like those of Chief Seattle's Suquamish people, were its only architectural heritage. Surely, here was a place from which to project the future, a place to form new words for a fresh language of architecture. In the twentieth century, from a desire to re-signify the world, modern architecture asserted itself with greater impact (negative and positive) than any other architecture.

The potential of the Northwest to ignite new aesthetic languages was magnified through the lens of painter Mark Tobey. Born in Wisconsin in 1890, by 1922 he had come to Seattle, the city with which he was chiefly associated for the next four decades.

As Piranesi is to Rome, Gauguin to Tahiti, or Hiroshige to Japan, so Tobey is to Seattle in his recording of a unique place fused with amazing invention. Tobey's paintings re-signify a world through the projection point of the Pacific Northwest.

The modern artist's necessary task of self-invention, however, did not emerge from a vacuum. Deep connections to the discipline of the art (or architecture) are crucial for development. Tobey had studied and traveled extensively in China and Japan, as well as in Europe, living for a time in a Kyoto monastery. His visits to the Far East led to his "calligraphic impulse," and thence to his mysterious "white writing" paintings that made him an internationally known abstract painter.

By curious coincidence, in 1946 painter Barnett Newman, the New York counterpoint of Tobey, organized a show in New York's Betty Parsons Gallery entitled "Northwest Coast Indian Painting." Parsons and Newman argued that Pacific Northwest art, wherein abstract design was far more than decorative, made a strong statement for the meaningfulness of modern art. Newman, a relentless curator for Northwest Coast Native painting, sought from New York's American Museum of Natural History, a large painted house façade that Newman felt was the closest in format to contemporary painting. He believed that the Northwest Coast Natives' sense of "pure painting" could be conveyed only with this piece of architecture.

From the abstractions native to the Pacific Northwest, the specific intensities of the architecture of Wendell Lovett and Arne Bystrom had fertile beginning ground.

While Grant Hildebrand and T. William Booth cover Lovett and Bystrom's work more thoroughly, I would like to reflect on two of their small works, which, like "seed-germs" or like Tobey's "white writing," radiate imagination and potential.

Wendell Lovett's retreat on Crane Island from 1970 is a tiny fusion of structure, landscape, and region. Slung between two wooden trusses, this minimalist, prefabricated house advances over an eroding saltwater beach typical of the Pacific Northwest. The particular image of site, sea, and house is so memorable that in my own student days at the University of Washington, it was the main image of an inspiring Northwest house, and it was created by one of our own professors of architecture.

The Raft River Retreat of Arne Bystrom also dating from 1970 is an eighteen-foot cube—pure architecture, comparable to Le Corbusier's artisans' house on the cover of *Verse Une Architecture* (1922). Le Corbusier's twenty-one-foot minimum house cube was to be built in straw mats sprayed with gunnite concrete inside and out. The interior had a single concrete column, which would also drain the roof.

Unlike the volumetrically pure planes of Le Corbusier's construction, Bystrom's cube was built of linear elements. A structural system of exposed lines of timber frame rests on round concrete point foundations. Sheathed in extra long cedar shakes over horizontal cedar boards, Bystrom's Raft River cubic volume has the surprise of a transparent roof. It is in the light of this transparent membrane that the parallels between the Raft River Retreat and Le Corbusier's artisans' house yield to a more distant relationship. I imagine a scene from those Pacific Northwest peoples in cedar plank longhouses, a thousand years before. The roofs of their houses were solid cedar shakes, perforated by a solitary central hole. In Bystrom's cube the roof is transparent, which creates an eighteen-by-eighteen-foot section of skylight; for aboriginal inhabitants the roof was one open hole for escaping smoke, which

surely caused a thickening of light. As Seattle's modernism continues to develop, it seems to emanate, at least in spirit, from this ancient thickened light.

Stretto House by Steven Holl, Dallas, Texas, 1991. The design is based on a compostion by Béla Bartók. (Courtesy of Paul Warchol Photography Inc.)

Preface

We are indebted, first of all, to Larry Woodin and Are Oyasaeter, who, as graduate students in the Department of Architecture at the University of Washington, wrote their theses on Wendell Lovett and Arne Bystrom, respectively, in 1979 and 1997. Specific citations of their work will be found in the text and notes. Additionally, Oyasaeter prepared and curated an exhibition of Bystrom's work at the Nordic Heritage Museum in Seattle, and arranged its subsequent appearance in his native Trondheim. Author T. William Booth assumed the lengthy task of organizing the collection of Bystrom material at the University of Washington's Northwest Collection, one of the Allen Library's Special Collections.

Valerie Broze Bystrom, Gilbert Eade, Leonard K. Eaton, Phillip Jacobson, Norman J. Johnston, Eileen Whitson Lovett, Brian McClaren, Jeffrey Karl Ochsner, and Daniel Streissguth read the manuscript at various points in its development and offered valuable criticism on both format and substance. In addition to a general critique of the text, Jeffrey Ochsner offered us the entirety of his meticulous research on Lionel Pries and the architecture program at Washington in Lovett's and Bystrom's time, and much of our relevant text is heavily indebted to Jeffrey's work. We are grateful also to the anonymous readers for the University of Washington Press, whose constructive comments led to many and major revisions. Wendell Lovett and Arne Bystrom opened their archives and searched their memories, while placing no

conditions of any kind on our use of their material. Many owners of the buildings discussed here have been unconditionally helpful. Among them we must especially thank Dr. Charles Simonyi for most courteously opening his Villa to us on several occasions, and Peggy and Reid Dennis for extending to us an open access to their home and for their warm and generous hospitality. We are much in their debt.

We are grateful to Marga Rose Hancock and the staff of AIA Seattle—the Seattle chapter of The American Institute of Architects—for their enthusiastic help in tracing many details of the two architects' professional careers, including their profusion of honors and awards.

Both Bystrom and Lovett have consistently documented their work in drawings, and in photographs of professional quality. We have incorporated those materials—or rather, a small selection of them, as the Appendix makes evident. We might have attempted a complete illustrated catalogue of each architect's work, but that would have meant either inadequate illustrations of centrally important examples or a formidable plethora of illustrations. It seemed to us that a concise selection of key examples, each quite fully illustrated and described, would best tell the story of their work. Accordingly, we have selected from each architect's career about eleven examples that we regard as most significant. The selection is not necessarily the one either architect would make, and we may well have omitted textual and pictorial material that future authors will wish to emphasize. All photographs without source identification are by either the architects or the authors and are credited in the Appendix; photographs from

Top: Wendell Lovett, VIlla Simonyi; bottom: Arne Bystrom, Dennis House.

other sources are credited appropriately in captions as they appear.

The cooperation of the credited professional photographers greatly assisted the recovery of original material. Thanks also to Heather Seneff, visual resources curator, College of Architecture and Urban Planning, and Nicolette Bromberg, visual materials curator, Special Collections of University of Washington Libraries.

Recognizing that the process of designing buildings involves talented staff we have acknowledged—wherever they are known—those who had important roles in the buildings discussed herein, and we have listed all known employees. The book is intended not only as a presentation and explication of its subject material, but also as an historical document; the appendix contains a chronological list of works by each architect, as well as awards and publications associated with each project.

Michael Duckworth, executive editor of the University of Washington Press, was enthusiastic in his support of this project from the time of our first discussions. He readily committed to a challenging standard of production quality and never wavered from that commitment. Managing editor Marilyn Trueblood kept us on course and allowed us time for important revisions. We sought a book design the reflected our subjects' modernist design ideas and Christina Merkelbach responded with a clean, intelligent layout. We are grateful to each of them for guidance and creative contributions.

We are solely responsible for any misrepresentation or misinterpretation of the material presented here.

Why do we have architecture? Why do we hire architects? The answer may lie in what Native Americans call the spirit, and in what the Chinese try to capture in feng shui—a need to harmonize the structure with some larger consideration, some integration of site, structure, and self. This innate ability, possessed by the few, draws forth some intangible subconscious realization and gives that realization a tangible form that brings us pleasure—in sounds, words, visual images, or architectural spaces. Such a pleasure also seems innate, and the subconscious intuitions it reflects probably once directed behaviors that yielded some survival advantage. If this is so, then music, poetry, art, and architecture are manifestations of such ineradicable ancient impulses. And if that, in turn, is so, then the intangible something these aesthetic expressions make tangible is a part of our well being. We value it because we need it. We are willing, even eager, to spend time, effort, and a good bit of money to have it. It is why we have architecture, and why we hire architects.

—Gilbert Eade

1.1 Wendell Lovett,
the Lovetts' vacation
retreat on Crane
Island, Washington,
1970.

A Prologue

Modernism, as the word relates to architecture, has existed in many versions, with many ostensible origins. All versions have had certain characteristics in common.

They turned firmly away from historic architectural styles. There are both negative and positive reasons for this. In the United States, by the late nineteenth century, Thoreau, Emerson, and Greenough had implicitly or explicitly argued the absurdity of stylistic revivals, while in Europe the flaws of several governments of ancient lineage—flaws increasingly evident after 1914—argued the folly of further allegiance to the past. More positively, the Industrial Revolution brought with it new building materials and methods, new structural possibilities, and new building types—especially the factory, the railroad station and train shed, and the high-rise commercial building. By the turn of the twentieth century these events were dramatically evidenced in America by the Brooklyn Bridge and Chicago's skyscrapers; in England by its many train sheds, the Crystal Palace and Telford's and Brunel's bridges; in France by the Bon Marché and the Eiffel Tower; and in Germany by the factories and industrial artifacts of Peter Behrens. Such events argued the inappropriateness of historic precedent, and that argument was embraced by all the various versions of modern architecture as they evolved over the next several decades.

Likewise, and for reasons implicit in the above paragraph, all versions of modernism maintained that the methods and materials of industrial society, and the purposes the designed artifact was to serve, should inform the design process and should be evident, in some way, in the physical result.

All versions also asserted that the purposes and dispositions of the building's interior spaces should be the paramount determinants of the design, and that ideally the exterior should be an uncompromised expression of the interior or, at the least, exterior and interior should not contradict one another.

All versions of modernism claimed to be founded on an objective chain of reasoning. All were argued with evangelical fervor and all claimed exclusive possession of the field. As anyone familiar with the various polemics will recall, there was in each case one way to design. The client and the world, if reluctant, must be persuaded. Any reasonable and open-minded person must see—or be made to see—the rational force of the argument.

Most versions of modernism verbally denied the legitimacy of ornament, though with varying degrees of conviction, and largely, one suspects, because of its associations with stylistic revivals. In their work, as opposed to their words, most modernists made their separate peace with the issue. Louis Sullivan and Frank Lloyd Wright found their own paths to an ornamentation that was often very rich indeed. It could be argued that Le Corbusier's late buildings, and Marcel Breuer's as well, are sculpture at an architectural scale. Mies van der Rohe made a kind of minimalist sculpture out of structure and detail, and in this, as he perhaps realized, he had a good bit of precedent, for structure and detail have been the wellsprings of ornament for many periods of architecture.

Some versions of modernism emphasized

technology, or perhaps technology and programmatic purpose, as the paramount determinants of design, and gave notably less attention to human emotional responses. There are understandable historic reasons for this, but in the first half of the twentieth century this issue became something of a dividing line between two camps of modernism, each including within itself several doctrines, but each relatively united on this issue. The technological-emphasis camp, if we may call it that, was largely European; it included many key figures of the Bauhaus and, in his early days, Le Corbusier.[1] Those modernists who were equally dedicated to the emotional dimension, on the other hand, seem to have been primarily American and Scandinavian. Among names of the first rank they include Sullivan and Wright, Alvar Aalto, and Eliel Saarinen, and among the slightly less well known, Bernard Maybeck, Charles and Henry Greene, Gunnar Asplund, Ralph Erskine, and Rolf Gutbrod. Among literary figures, Lewis Mumford comes immediately to mind.

Wendell Lovett and Arne Bystrom began their careers at a time when European modernism—often simply called modernism or Modernism—was predominant. Lovett's professional life in his native Seattle, and his teaching career at the University of Washington, began in 1948. Fellow Seattle native Arne Bystrom, one of Lovett's first students, graduated in 1951. The European modernist influence is fully evident in the earliest work of both men. In the decades to follow, however, modernism in its many versions was severely reexamined, and architecture, in theory and practice, was beset and reshaped by a series of polemics.[2] Throughout this lengthy time of challenge and reform, Lovett and Bystrom never abandoned basic modernist tenets. But neither are any of their mature works simple reiterations of early modernism. Four of their buildings, spanning a period of twenty-five years, will illustrate some of the parallels in their work, as well as some of the distinctions.

In 1970 Lovett designed a vacation retreat

1.2 Arne Bystrom, the Bystroms' Raft River cabin on the Washington coast, 1970-78. The cabin from the northwest.

for his family, on one of the smallest of the San Juan Islands off the northwest coast of Washington. Its most evident and dramatic feature is the deck that hovers above the beach, held between two seemingly inverted trusses poised on the edge of the bluff. The tiny retreat includes only a kitchen, a bath, and sitting and sleeping areas, contained within the opaque walls that withdraw into the trees.

In the same year, Bystrom began an equally small project for the same purpose, a shingled cube with a glass roof, at the edge of the forest above Washington's Pacific coast. Various platforms inside define kitchen, dining, and living spaces, with sleeping lofts above. From these spaces wooden decks without rails reach outward into the trees, and westward toward the edge of the continent. The Bystrom family built the retreat themselves, finishing it in 1978.

Four years later Bystom began the design of a home for Peggy and Reid Dennis in Sun Valley, Idaho, that is as large as the coastal retreat is small. The house utilizes state-of-the-art solar energy technology, and within and along the southern walls, under three planes of roof and behind the great wooden columns, is a continuous sunlit space that encompasses the devices of the energy system. Beyond, under the north side of the roof, is a building within a building, a two-story composition that includes the dining space, kitchen, five bedrooms, the garage, and a caretaker's suite. This building-within-a-building, the stairs that serve it, and the roof that protects it, are astonishing exercises in wood detailing and craftsmanship. The Dennis house was completed in 1986.

In 1987 Lovett began the design of a home for Charles Simonyi on a waterfront site near Seattle. The first phase, with the usual domestic spaces, is now the central portion of the Villa Simonyi; additions after 1993 tripled its size. The northern addition includes a pool at

1.3 Bystrom, the Peggy and Reid Dennis house, Sun Valley, Idaho, 1982-86. The exterior from the south. (© Michael Jensen)

1.4 Dennis house. The interior, looking east. The "building within a building" is center and left; the helical stair accesses the upper guest bedroom. The southern sunlit volume is at the extreme right.

and relationships in which Lovett has long believed.

These buildings derive from a modernist attitude toward program and structure, choice and usage of materials, relationship of interior and exterior, and avoidance of historic stylistic sources; in these respects they illustrate the most durable tenets of modernism. At the same time, they are far indeed from any midcentury examples of those tenets, including the earliest work of either Lovett or Bystrom. Rather, the four buildings exemplify an enriched and thriving modernism the two architects have evolved over the five decades of their careers, each in his own way, through his own predilections and his own processes of growth and change.

On some matters Lovett and Bystrom have reached similar destinations. As remarkably thoughtful composers of spaces, they have arrived at a shared set of spatial characteristics and compositions that seem to have a demonstrable human appeal. They share a passion for expressive detail, executed through extraordinary craftsmanship, and a deep belief in the emotional dimension of architecture. Both have spent their lives in Seattle; all of their projects are in the Pacific Northwest;[3] most have been residential. Both architects have been favored with exceptional sites on which to build.

On other matters they differ, and on those matters the work of each illuminates the distinctive characteristics of the other. For Lovett, intuition is the raw material of introspection and cognitive examination; Bystrom's intuitions find their way more directly to the drawing board. Lovett's work has long been influenced by that of several twentieth-century Scandinavian architects, while Bystrom's is increasingly informed by images of ancient Scandinavian stave churches. Lovett is dedicated to high-tech expressionism; Bystrom's passion is wood. Yet it is not so easy to say

grade, an exercise suite above, children's rooms on the third level, and a master suite on the fourth level, cantilevering toward the water. The southern wing is a gallery for a considerable art collection. Architect and client share an admiration for the paintings of Vasarely and Lichtenstein, and an affection for technology—hence the project's several geometric themes and its technically luxurious details. The Villa also shares with Bystrom's Dennis house a canon of spatial configurations

which is the romantic and which the rational-ist: Lovett's dedication to industrialized materials and methods is informed by gesture and anthropomorphic metaphor; Bystrom, devoted to the natural and the handcrafted, works from the abstract disciplines of geom-etry and physics, invariably manifested in a crisp, concise structural idea.

The two architects, compatriots and colleagues for half a century, and with half a century of honors and awards, are still in active practice in Seattle. Lovett continues to manipu-late space, light, and mechanistic inspiration, with a richness undreamed of in the early days of modernism, while Bystrom's celebration of wood as an informing idea is comparable to that of Greene and Greene a century ago, or to ancient Asian crafts. Their remarkable careers deserve to be better known.

1.5 Lovett, the Charles Simonyi house, Villa Simonyi, Medina, Washington, 1987–. The exterior from Lake Washing-ton. The original villa is at center; the gallery is above the boat. The glass-enclosed pool is at far left, at grade.

1.6 Lovett, the Villa Simonyi. The interior of the original phase, looking north. The breakfast space is in the foreground; above, beyond the glass wall, is the small gallery. Lake Washington is at left. (© Michael Jensen)

2.1 Lovett, third year design studio analytique, 1942, deriving from the teaching methodology of the École des Beaux-Arts; a watercolor representation of a building and its detail features, canonically arranged as a formal composition.

Wendell Lovett's Formative Years

Pearl Harper's father was a patternmaker and toolmaker who, lured by the Klondike Gold Rush, got as far as Seattle. Wallace Lovett's father had founded a Seattle preservative coatings and roofing firm, to which Wallace was heir. Wallace and Pearl married in 1918; Wendell Harper Lovett, their only child, was born on April 2, 1922.

As a child Wendell was obsessed with mechanical things, including a beloved pedal car somehow modified by a neighbor to make it "better."[1] He remembers his grandfather's "big machine shop." He remembers going to Boeing Field with his father, and the "biplanes and the guy wires and the tension of the fabric over the ribs";[2] he thinks, perhaps, he touched Lindbergh's *Spirit of St. Louis* when it landed at Seattle's Sand Point. His childhood also included the arts. The Lovetts had perennial season tickets to the Seattle Symphony and a serious collection of records of classical music, and Wendell was taken to movies and vaudeville in the fantasy interiors of the Pantages theaters, designed by Seattle architect Marcus Priteca. He remembers a large half-timber house in his neighborhood—architect Henry Bittman's own house, actually—that brought the realization that architects create such things. In the eighth grade he was taken on a field trip to the University of Washington's school of architecture. The design studio, like all others before and since, would have been filled with exhausted but intense students, models everywhere, drawings in line and exotic color on every desk and wall. And the ambience at the time of Wendell's visit must have been even more extravagantly impressive than usual, because the year was 1936, and the school then included a number of students of quite extraordinary ability.[3] Wendell decided that day to be an architect, and throughout his high school years he stayed with his decision.

In the spring of 1940, Wendell's senior year, the University's Henry Art Gallery exhibited the work of the renowned Finnish architect Alvar Aalto.[4] Future events suggest that Wendell may have seen the exhibit, but he has no memory of doing so. He entered the University's program in architecture that fall.

At the time, there were a few American schools of architecture that, in individualistic ways, explicitly claimed to address design purposes and processes appropriate to the unique conditions of the mid-twentieth century. Eliel Saarinen's Cranbrook Academy of Art in southwestern Michigan, begun in the mid-1920s, was one of the earliest of these. Wright's Taliesin Fellowship, in Wisconsin and Arizona, formally constituted as a school in the early 1930s, was foremost in notoriety, though small in numbers of students. W. R. B. Willcox, a Chicago native and Wright's contemporary, who had supported the founding of the program at Washington, taught a gentler version of the Chicago and Prairie School philosophy at the University of Oregon from 1922 to 1947.

The vast majority of architectural schools in the United States in the mid-1940s, however, drew, in varying degrees, from two dominant teaching models. The Parisian École des Beaux-Arts, in America often simply called "the École," based its instruction on canonical principles of spatial and formal composition, supported by a firm grasp of pre-nineteenth-

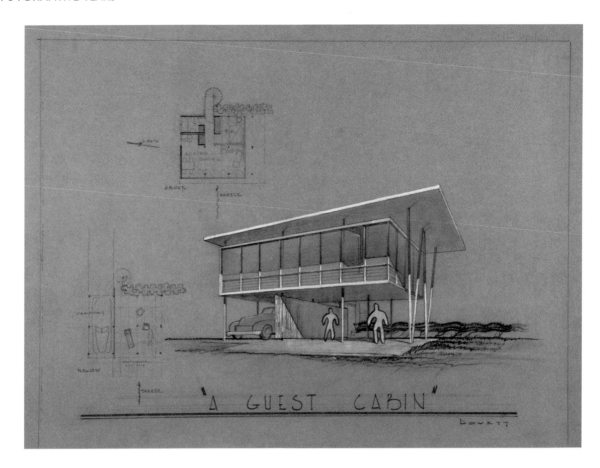

2.2 Lovett, fourth-year design studio eight-hour sketch problem, 1946: "A Guest Cabin."

century historic examples. Teaching was in *ateliers*—studios—of renowned Parisian architects. By the early twentieth century the *atelier* instruction followed a canonical process. A problem having been assigned, each student, in an intense eight-hour *esquisse en loge*, would derive a *parti*, a basic design scheme. This *parti* would then be developed by the student, without significant departure in configuration or character, over the ensuing weeks and months, with ongoing *critique* by the master of the *atelier*. The final presentation included elaborate renderings, usually in watercolor and often in the form of an *analytique,* a formally arranged composition on a large sheet or board depicting the overall building and several key details at various scales. The École method was in widespread use in American schools from the early years of the century, although the *atelier*[5] was typically replaced by an on-campus studio, a large space with a sizable drafting board and sideboard for each of the several students. Many American schools still followed the Ecole model through the 1940s; a few retained it, or elements of it, into the early 1950s.

But from the late 1920s the German Bauhaus—in Weimar, then Dessau, then Berlin—was increasingly influential. It held that a design methodology appropriate to the mid-twentieth century must derive from the nature of the problem and the means and materials of the time; hence, unlike the École, it did not teach history at all. The Bauhaus further held that students could not develop a design methodology by learning canonical composi-tional principles, but must work directly with contemporary materials and methods, in carefully structured exercises, to discover their intrinsic characteristics, thereby deriving appropriate new design methods, applications, usages, and forms. By the late 1930s several examples of American architecture reflected the influence of the Bauhaus, and three major Bauhaus faculty had come to America: Ludwig Mies van der Rohe was at Chicago's Armour Institute, soon to be the Illinois Institute of Technology; Walter Gropius and Marcel Breuer were at Harvard. In the years immediately following the war, the philosophy they represented rapidly spread to other American schools, and came to pervade the profession. That philosophy, often coupled with the work and thought of Le Corbusier, might now most clearly be termed "European modernism."

Washington's program during Wendell's years could not be fully described in terms of any of these philosophies, largely because of its dominant faculty member, Lionel Henry "Spike" Pries (1897-1968).[6] Pries, a native of California, had studied in École-based programs at Berkeley and the University of Pennsylvania, where in 1920 he worked directly under Paul Cret, dean of American advocates of the École. After graduation in 1921, Pries also assisted Cret in evening instruction at the T-Square Club, whose "atelier" taught draftsmen who were unable to enroll in an architecture school. Pries's early reputation in design, and perhaps in teaching, was such that he was offered a position at Washington in 1923 by Carl Gould, founder and head of the department, and campus architect and planner as well.[7] In 1928, having negotiated what was then a very generous salary, Pries moved to Seattle to join the faculty as instructor. At the same time he formed an architectural partnership with Penn classmate William Bain, and by 1930 he had also accepted a position as curator of the Art Institute of Seattle (later the Seattle Art Museum).

Pries possessed an impressive knowledge of the arts of Europe, of course, but also of Native America, the Far East, South Asia and Africa, the Art Deco and the Moderne, and he spent many of his summers in Mexico, where he saw the work of Diego Rivera, Miguel Covarrubias, and Juan O'Gorman. In his classes on the history of ornament, and above all in his studio teaching, he drew from this remarkably broad knowledge of examples and principles. By the late 1930s he had also apprised himself of the beliefs and work of the Bauhaus—although he despised its teaching methods—and he respected and had increasingly accepted much European and American modernist work and thought. He encouraged his students to explore equally catholic interests.[8] Throughout Pries's entire career at Washington, however, he taught by means of the École methodology.

Pries's dedication to his profession and his students extended far beyond scheduled classroom and studio instruction; he was often in the studios during evening and weekend hours, discussing and sketching. As presentation dates approached he usually appeared in the studios more frequently, bringing his watercolor equipment, to work alongside the students, brush in hand, on their *analytiques*. And several times in every term he opened his home to them for evening gatherings. There he introduced them to classical music—he had an extensive collection of records and a superb record player—and gave them free rein to explore his library and his remarkable selection of works of art.

Wendell was influenced by Pries's teaching as well as his aura. Pries reinforced Wendell's early fondness for the visual arts and music, and later events suggest that Pries instilled in Wendell, as in so many students at Washington, an unusually open attitude toward a breadth of influences. Wendell's work in his first years in the program reveals Pries's impress, within a body of projects that are often excellent representatives of the École approach. And Wendell still has, and clearly treasures, many books bought in those early years, at Pries's suggestion, that reveal a richly romantic view of architectural examples and architectural rendering techniques. And yet, even in Wendell's early years in the program, students at Washington, as elsewhere, were beginning to bring modernist influences into their studio design work, and Pries did not discourage them from doing so.

In April 1943, Wendell's third year, he was called into the Army. He went to Normandy with the 13th Armored Division in early 1945 and served until the war in Europe ended. After a brief holiday in Paris he returned to a base in California, to be discharged in February 1946. He reentered the University.

Wendell's studio projects of his last two years more consistently reflect modernist influences, to which he seems to have become more intensely dedicated than many of his classmates. He would have heard modernist work and thought increasingly discussed in the school, informally in studios, and formally, to some extent, even in classrooms. And he had found and read G. E. Kidder-Smith's *Brazil Builds*, and Le Corbusier's *Complete Works* and *When the Cathedrals Were White*: "I discovered [Le Corbusier] through sneaky trips to the library—these things were buried in a corner

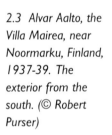

2.3 Alvar Aalto, the Villa Mairea, near Noormarku, Finland, 1937-39. The exterior from the south. (© Robert Purser)

somewhere—didn't look like anyone had ever touched them."[9] Though Wendell's surviving school drawings contain no particular Corbusian references, he ranks Le Corbusier first among his early architectural heroes. He had also learned of at least some of the work of Alvar Aalto, either from the Henry Gallery exhibit of his senior high school year, or from his more recent library burrowings, or both. And at this same time, presumably in these same library burrowings, he remembers having discovered material on the bridges and buildings of the Swiss engineer Robert Maillart that illustrated Maillart's integration of the mathematical and the intuitive.

Wendell graduated in June 1947, at or near the top of his class, and was awarded the AIA Silver Medal.[10] He decided to pursue graduate study, and was accepted at Harvard and the Massachusetts Institute of Technology. He knew that Aalto had recently designed the Baker House residence hall for MIT, and was in Cambridge to supervise its construction, and he chose that school in the hope that Aalto might also teach there in the coming year.

While on leave from the Army in 1945, he had met Eileen Whitson at a Seattle Symphony concert. She had been a soloist with the San Francisco Opera Ballet and the New York Dance Players; her father's death had brought her back to her native Seattle. Wendell and Eileen were married on September 3, 1947, and the next day left Seattle for Cambridge and MIT.

As Wendell had guessed, Aalto was serving as visiting professor. Although Wendell's submission for a two-day sketch problem late in the year won the William R. Ware Prize, some other work fared less well. Early in the year the students were given a two-week project, to be done without critiques, for a major office complex sited anywhere in the United States at the student's

choice. Wendell chose Boston's beloved Copley Square, and proposed at its edge a prismatic office tower with subordinate elements suggesting Le Corbusier's UN Building.[11] Wendell may have been encouraged in this direction by Ralph Rapson of the MIT faculty, who was then a devotee of Le Corbusier, and for whose firm Wendell was working. But Aalto was to critique the completed projects, and he had long since found his own direction, sharply different from that of either the Bauhaus or Le Corbusier. His most representative project to that date was perhaps the Villa Mairea of 1938-39, a home in the Finnish countryside, the antithesis of the prototypical, deeply specific to its place—a work both gentler and more complex than could be found, or even envisioned, in canonical European modernism. Aalto was not impressed with Wendell's Copley Square proposal; he considered it too cold, too grand, and too impersonal. He also regarded without enthusiasm Wendell's later equally Corbusian thesis project for housing, disagreeing with the inclusion of terraces within the body of the project. He suggested stepping the upper floors to create terraces open to the sun—a suggestion Wendell felt, and still feels, was wrong for Boston's climate. He remembers thinking after one critique that "Aalto seemed to make arbitrary choices, which were beyond my grasp. I don't think I really was ready to appreciate his viewpoint, nor did I understand it."[12] But Aalto's critiques sowed in Wendell the seeds of alternative ways of thinking about design.

So did Aalto's Baker House, which Wendell photographed extensively. Baker House is modernist in the crisp geometry of its dining hall, its absence of historic reference, and its occasional imaginative use of twentieth-century materials. But it is far from European modernism in the handmade character of its brickwork, its undulating facade toward the

2.4 Villa Mairea. West end of exterior. (© Robert Purser)

2.5 Villa Mairea. The stair from the living room. (© Robert Purser)

2.6 *Villa Mairea. The dining room. (© Robert Purser)*

2.7 *Aalto, the Baker House Residence Hall, Massachusetts Institute of Technology, Cambridge, 1947-48. The exterior from the north. (© Stephen Friedlaender)*

2.8 *Baker House; interior of a student room. (© MIT Museum)*

river, its unprecedented north facade, its corridors that are more social streets than corridors, and the intimate ambience of its student rooms. As such it, and Aalto himself, were well outside the conceptual framework that Wendell and, for that matter, most of the contemporaneous architectural profession were then following. Furthermore, Wendell was beginning to think about systems building for housing, and in that context Baker House seemed too handcrafted, too labor intensive, "quirky and strange, almost medieval. I didn't really understand the quality of space, the feeling, the humanistic aspect of what Aalto achieved there."[13] Wendell would remember Aalto's words, and Aalto's work, and would revisit them creatively and at length, but only after a considerable time of gestation.

Lovett finished the program at MIT in June 1948. He and Eileen made a brief celebratory trip to New York, where he happened on a copy of *Domus,* the serial publication of Italian design, that would leave a lasting impression. On his return to Seattle he worked for two months for the firm of Naramore, Bain, Brady and Johanson, for whom he had worked the previous summer; he then accepted a job with Bassetti and Morse, Architects. Fred Bassetti was a recent graduate of Harvard, where Walter Gropius then held sway, and Bassetti was immersed in the problem of the lower-

cost single family house made from standard components, a problem on which Gropius and Conrad Wachsmann had spent years of study.[14] Bassetti encouraged Lovett in this interest, and immediately gave him considerable design responsibility. Some fireplaces in the houses the firm was doing were designed with sheet-metal hoods, and Lovett, in preparing contract drawings for these, began to study a design for a prefabricated factory-made version. This study would ultimately become the "Firehood."

Bassetti also subscribed to *Domus* and encouraged Lovett to dog-ear the office's copies. Lovett soon subscribed for himself. The journal had been re-founded in January 1946 by Ernesto Rogers to address the reconstruction of family homes destroyed in the war (hence its subtitle "the house of man"). An article by Vittorio Gandolfini in the initial volume epitomized the journal's early purpose: Gandolfini proposed an efficient low-cost apartment for a working-class family, including seven new pieces of furniture that could be home-built or factory-produced inexpensively. *Domus* thus reinforced Lovett's stated interests at MIT and supported his work with Bassetti.[15] In its pages Lovett would discover and follow, over the years, the work of Franco Albini, Carlo Molino, Gio Ponti, Carlo Scarpa, and especially Ernesto Rogers.

That same fall Lovett was offered a half-time teaching position at the University.[16] He accepted, with Bassetti's regretful but gracious support, reducing his hours at the office. He was intrinsically interested in teaching, and he believed, too, that his own professional growth would benefit from continuing contact with young designers-in-training.

Lovett also joined a group that included both Bassetti and partner Jack Morse,[17] to build a planned community east of Lake Washington, to be called The Hilltop Community. There he built his first house, in 1950-51,

2.9 *The Architecture faculty at the University of Washington, in 1951. Lovett is second from the right (in front); Lionel Pries is at the back, in front of the window. Others include Victor Steinbrueck (back row, dark hair); to Lovett's left, Omer Mithun; to Lovett's right, Jack Sproule; in the middle (arms crossed), Myer Wolfe; fourth from top left, George Tsutakawa. (© University of Washington College of Architecture and Urban Planning Archives)*

for Eileen and himself. The Hilltop house reveals none of Lovett's earlier allegiance to Le Corbusier, little of Aalto,[18] and a major influence from Mies van der Rohe. In the early 1950s almost all frequently published American architects except Frank Lloyd Wright were working in a Miesian idiom,[19] and this may account, in part, for the character of the Hilltop house. But Lovett had also just read Albert Frey's *In Search of a Living Architecture*,[20] a book directly and indirectly supportive of Mies, and, additionally, a paean to architecture as technology. Lovett remembers it as "a compact bit of prose and graphics with a powerful message."[21] Frey proposed that "modern structures and natural settings are direct opposites, a contrast which emphasizes the precise appearance of the building and the irregular expression of nature, to the advantage of both."[22] Other propositions reinforced Lovett's own fondness for industrial forms and devices: "New structural systems use skeletal frames, take advantage of tensile strength in materials, and combine frames with stressed coverings. . . . [A light steel] framework lets us visualize the exterior shape and the interior space simultaneously . . ."[23] and "[mass produced] products, though independently created, achieve unity of expression through a similarity of intention."[24] With Frey's words much in his mind, and *Domus*'s mission as well, Lovett designed the Hilltop project as a prototype of a technologically sophisticated

2.10 Lovett, the Wendell and Eileen Lovett house, "Hilltop," Bellevue, 1950-51; plan.

2.11 Hilltop house. The exterior from the southeast.

2.12 Hilltop house. The interior.

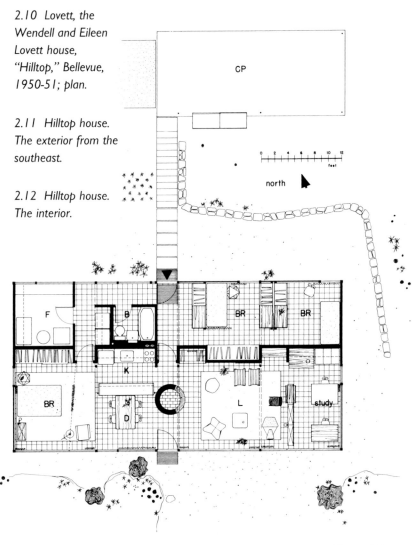

house that a young family might build by themselves: "I was always thinking, at this time, of things that could be produced as components and assembled with basic tools."[25] The house was published, both at home and abroad, as a prototype of the minimalist dwelling.[26]

In these years Lovett worked at Bassetti and Morse in the mornings, taught in the afternoons, and spent his evenings either doing competitions or designing furniture. The only available furniture he liked he could not afford, so he was designing for his own use, but with mass production also in mind.[27] In 1949 he had begun work on a lounge chair, whose base would be a tripod of steel rods supporting a plastic shell cut from a flat sheet, then shaped and clipped, to create a three-dimensional ergonomic form to which foam pads would be applied. A fabric or leather "bikini" was then to be laced to the shell. He built several prototypes—one was exhibited in Domus's home city, Milan, at the 1954 Triennale—and used the design in several houses. It is still in limited production and is still strikingly elegant; the design has worn well. In this same period he completed the design of the "Firehood" fireplace with singly curved sheet-metal hood and cast-iron hearth, patented it, and in 1954 licensed its manufacture by Condon-King Company Inc.

In the same year Lovett completed a house for his parents that was very much like his own. In the process of its design and construction he began to feel less comfortable with his technical preoccupations. His thoughts were increasingly turning toward questions of human emotional need, and the ways in which such questions might more effectively inform his architecture. In his next house, in 1955, for Gervais and Connie Reed, also of the Hilltop community, Lovett began to modify his formal and spatial vocabulary. The Reed plan remains completely rectilinear, but diagonal elements in section and elevation provide both lateral rigidity and a richer sculptural profile. The house marks Lovett's first exploration into ideas of open and closed, opaque and transparent: while light and outlook are provided by considerable areas of glass wall, spaces are contained and defined by prevalent opaque surfaces. Lovett saw the house as "an opportunity to explore non-Miesian expression; I discovered enclosure and containment."[28] In a

second house for his parents, built in 1957, Lovett abandoned forever the glazed Miesian prism. In plan, sections, and elevations, angles other than 90 degrees suggested embracing enclosure; exterior walls were gently angular and dominantly opaque. Four similar houses followed in the same year.

Thus Lovett began to revise his fundamental architectural purposes and means, and so too his communicative means were changing. At the time of his return from MIT, he had begun using hand gestures to describe architectural characteristics; in working through the projects of the late 1950s he increasingly used such gestures to frame and express ideas. Bassetti, who remained a friend and professional confidant, remembers Lovett's hands continually enfolding and shaping, gesturing to frontness and backness of the body, to open and closed, to containment and release—a habit Lovett retains to this day. His words,

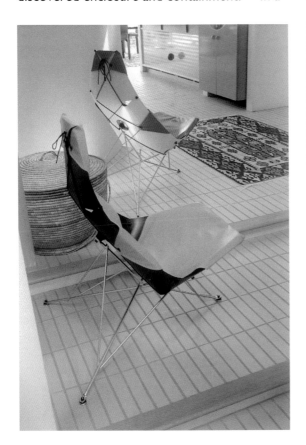

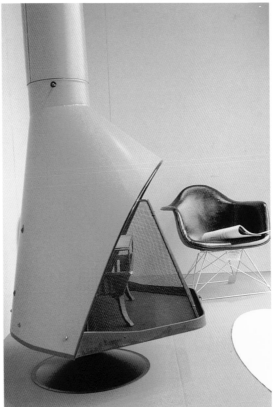

2.13 Lovett, the "Flexifibre," later "Bikini," chair. First seen at the Milan Triennale of 1954; handsome, remarkably comfortable, and still in production.

2.14 Lovett, the "Firehood." The beginning of an industry.

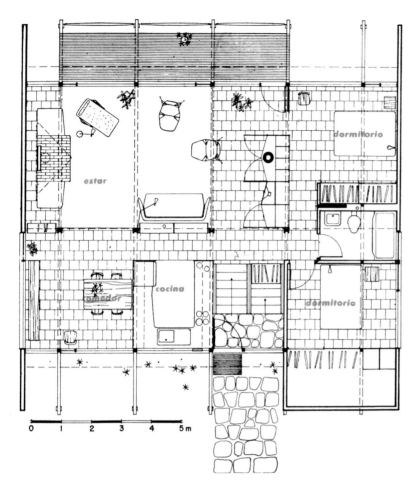

too, were at this time moving away from descriptions of mechanistic and industrial intentions and toward the exploration of spatial and formal metaphors: "We tend to put spaces on; we wrap them around us, putting the openings—the eyes of the building—in front, enclosure behind. The house can be thought of as the last in a chain of personal body-shell extensions. . . . The most communicative forms are usually those that are concave, broken, serrated, those that wrap or enclose the body."[29]

That same year, Arthur Herrman, the Director of the School of Architecture at Washington, discussed with Wolfgang Henning of the Technical Institute of Stuttgart an exchange of young faculty, as a result of which Peter Schenk, an assistant to Rolf Gutbrod, came to Washington in 1959 as a Visiting Instructor. Lovett was his faculty host. In the exchange Gutbrod endorsed Lovett for a Fulbright grant as guest critic at Stuttgart for the academic year 1959-60.[30] The year would be a memorable one.

Among a diverse faculty at Stuttgart,

2.15 Lovett, Gervais and Connie Reed house, Bellevue, WA, 1955. Plan.

2.16 Reed house. The exterior.

Lovett found in Gutbrod an almost ideal stimulus. Gutbrod was seeking an alternative to the regimented academic climate inherited from the years between the wars. He felt that the spaces of what he would call an "organic architecture" might be molded as needs would suggest. So far this was canonical modernism, but for Gutbrod, needs must include emotional needs. Cognitive thought and rational analysis could not exclusively shape architectural decisions; intuition might have an equally valid claim. Gesture, because it is immediate and universal, might be more fundamental than language and, because gesture is visual, it might more appropriately determine and find expression in architectural form. An architecture that would emerge from these ideas might embody visual conflict as well as accord, if these appropriately represented the character and use of each of the various spaces, and the lives of their occupants. And Gutbrod, a master violinist, enlarged Lovett's interest in music, including its structural and perceptual analogies to architecture; Gutbrod spoke of architecture as counterpoint, thus more complex, even atonal.

Others at Stuttgart were interested in redressing the separation between civil engineering and architecture; their champion was Fritz Leonhardt, director of the Institute for Concrete Structures, and a pioneer in pretensioned concrete systems. Leonhardt was especially interested in clearly articulating tensile elements as distinct from those in compression; Lovett would specifically adopt this interest. During this trip he also attended a lecture by the Swedish architect Ralph Erskine, whose work Lovett knew and admired through its publication in *Domus*. Erskine had explored nonrectilinear plan forms, using freely disposed wall alignments and, often, curved corners; he argued their validity as in part a response to the harsh Swedish climate, and in part the sort of anthropomorphic

expression Lovett was himself contemplating.

Thus at Stuttgart, away from the distractions of practice, and among stimulating colleagues reflecting in various ways on a number of cognate issues, Lovett began to consolidate his thoughts. Hindsight suggests that as he did so he was increasingly reminded, consciously or subconsciously, of Aalto's buildings and Aalto's words.

Immediately on his return to Seattle in 1960, Lovett, in collaboration with Seattle architect Ted Bower, was engaged in the design of a pedestrian walkway shelter system for the Seattle Century 21 Exposition planned for 1962.[31] The design reflects Lovett's interest in the autonomous expression of tensile and compressive forces, an interest that was encouraged by his contact with Leonhardt at Stuttgart. The little Century 21 umbrellas are not well remembered, even in Seattle, but they were surely among the most engaging structures of the Exposition.

The Lovetts had become a family of four: daughter Corrie was born in 1951, Clare in 1954. The Hilltop house was small, with little privacy; Lovett had wanted to enlarge it for some time. On his return from Stuttgart, he saw that he might do so by means of a markedly different spatial and formal character. The

2.17 Reed house. The interior; the living room. The roof beams express the concentration of forces in upper and lower edges; the fireplace continues Lovett's exploration in sheet-metal fabrication. Two "Bikini" chairs are at right.

2.18 Lovett, "umbrellas" for the Century 21 Exposition, Seattle, 1961. A manifestation of Lovett's Stuttgart association with Fritz Leonhardt.

remodeling would occupy him through 1963.

The western half of the original house would be the girls' domain, with the original entry as their private entry. The entire eastern half would be the new living space. North of it new excavation would provide an alcove from the living space, and a studio and shop. Lovett imagined the living space and its alcove as the upturned palm of a hand. Above it he would place, metaphorically, another hand, palm downward, that would envelop a carport and a new entry, a master bedroom, a kitchen, and a dining space. Of these spaces, a full floor above the original floor plane, the dining space, and to a lesser extent the kitchen, would overlook the new living space below. Connection from the upper level to the lower would be by means of a helical stair.

The configuration of the addition could hardly be more different from that of the original house. Ninety-degree relationships are rare. Bounding surfaces are almost entirely opaque. The exterior is not a direct revelation

of the interior. The most fundamental difference, however, is volumetric: instead of simple prismatic volumes, kitchen, dining, living, and alcove spaces are a sequence of subspaces within a single complex bounding envelope. These subspaces are articulated by the architectural furniture of cabinetwork, balcony, and stair, yet they also partake of one another, and are expressed as doing so by the undulating ceiling that sweeps over them all.

Aalto's influence appears here clearly for the first time, twelve years after Lovett's MIT experiences, in the juxtaposition of white surfaces and natural materials, and in the occasional free form of an element within an otherwise crisp geometry. This is most evident in the exquisite cedar ceiling, by no means simply the undersurface of the roof, which inevitably suggests the auditorium in Aalto's library at Viipuri. The metaphorical gesture of clasped hands may have come from Lovett's Stuttgart experiences. The stair, however, owes nothing to either Aalto or Stuttgart. It

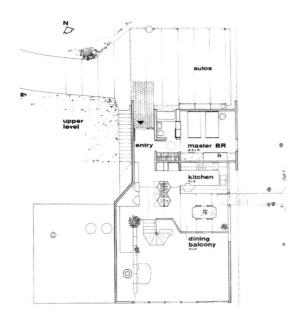

does reveal Lovett's continuing interest in contemporaneous Italian design, an interest that—like the stair itself—is a manifestation of his lifelong fascination with mechanistic geneses of form. That mechanistic fascination, however, is here no longer an end in itself but an element within a larger experiential context.

The path of movement from the entry, past the bedroom, kitchen, and dining spaces and down the stair to the living space, passes through none of those designated spaces on its journey. Lovett will begin to call this a "go" space. And none of the designated spaces accessed by the "go" space replicates its role: bedroom, kitchen, dining, and living spaces are dead-ended, serving no purpose of circulation to other spaces. Lovett will call these "stop" spaces. The remodeled Hilltop scheme can be seen to be a composition of clearly differentiated "stop" and "go" spaces. The differentiation frees the "stop" spaces of any mandatory circulation purpose; they can be spaces of uncompromised repose. In this, the remodeling is sharply different from the original scheme, whose kitchen, dining, and living spaces intentionally included circulation.

The redesigned living space is large in all dimensions. It receives a considerable quantity of light, from the original south glazing but also

2.19 Lovett, the Hilltop remodeling, Bellevue, 1961-63. The exterior from the northwest; the carport and entry are at extreme left, with kitchen clerestory just visible at top left center.

2.20 Hilltop remodeling. Plans and section through the living space, dining balcony, and the cave.

from windows to the east and, in the distance, from the kitchen's north clerestory. The space offers extensive interior views across its own considerable dimensions, and to dining and kitchen, and into the little alcove under the dining balcony. It also offers an exterior view to the northeast, another to the northern sky through the kitchen clerestory, and a view of many miles' extent to the south. The contiguous alcove under the dining balcony is opposite in every way. It is small in plan dimension, with a low ceiling; its walls are largely opaque; its surfaces are soft, tactile; views are of short reach; cozy seating wraps the sides visible from the larger space. Thus two opposite spatial conditions are juxtaposed. One—the living space proper—is large, bright, open, with extended views; the other—the alcove—is small, dark, containing. Each opens to the other and each can be seen from the other. Lovett will call these complementary spaces the "meadow" and the "cave."[32] He will make them ubiquitous features of his subsequent houses.

The character of the Hilltop remodeling is in part—perhaps in large measure—a consequence of the Stuttgart epiphany. But it may be no coincidence that elements of Aalto's formal vocabulary appear for the first time, as outward evidence of deeper analogies to his work and thought. For in the aftermath of Stuttgart, Lovett may well have recalled that Aalto too, in

2.21 Hilltop remodeling. The interior; the kitchen, with the dining balcony beyond.

2.22 Hilltop remodeling. The interior; the dining balcony.

his writings and his buildings, and in his critiques at MIT, had stressed the sensory dimension, the importance of intuition in design, the value of psychological considerations and biological analogies, and the emotional power of images of shelter and protection.

In the period that preceded and accompanied the Hilltop redesign, the very ubiquity of European modernism led many architects to seek ways of moving beyond its increasingly evident limitations. By 1960, Le Corbusier's revolutionary sculpture of mass, space, and light at Ronchamp had been widely published. In America, in the late 1950s, the delicate wooden modernism of Seattle's Paul Hayden Kirk was nationally recognized. In the middle of that decade Minoru Yamasaki, Kirk's University of Washington classmate, had explicitly declared his intention to enrich the Miesian canon; the MacGregor Center at Detroit's Wayne State University is the outstanding example from that period of his career. His work was widely known, and it certainly was known in Seattle, as Washington graduate Astra Zarina was a designer in Yamasaki's office, and Yamasaki was the dominant figure on the University's Design Committee. Eero Saarinen's TWA terminal at New York's Idlewild (now John F. Kennedy) Airport was finished in 1955, and his Dulles terminal outside Washington was accepted as a classic work on its completion in 1962, just after his premature death. Paul Rudolph's theatrical concrete Yale School of Architecture opened in 1960. In the following year, Louis I. Kahn's Richards Medical Laboratories at the University of Pennsylvania appeared in publication after publication. Articulated to

2.23 Hilltop remodeling. The interior; the meadow, looking toward the cave, and the dining balcony above.

23

2.24 Hilltop remodeling. The interior; the living space, looking east.

distinguish "master" and "servant" spaces, Kahn's building imaged some indeterminate future; yet its base suggested an ancient stylobate, while its brick walls and crenellated skyline recalled Albi, or Caernarvon. In the same year, Charles Moore designed a less publicized small house for himself in Orinda, California, whose neo-vernacular exterior of shingles and sliding barn doors enclosed an interior featuring two canopies on neo-Tuscan wood columns; Moore referred to them as Roman "aediculae." Moore intended this project to challenge what he, and others, had begun to regard as the restrictive dogmas of modernism. Other challenges would follow. In 1966, in *Complexity and Contradiction in Architecture*, Robert Venturi eloquently attacked a wide range of modernist tenets, advocating a

freedom of approach that could—should—include historic references, willfulness, irony, even whimsy.

No one actively involved in architecture at that time could be unaware of these events.[33] In design studios at the University, furthermore, Lovett would have been drawn into lengthy discussions of them all, including Venturi's book when it was published; it immediately captured wide attention among both students and faculty. But Lovett would only occasionally adopt influences from these and other later challenges to modernism. To a far greater degree than his colleagues, he kept himself informed about the work and thought of other less widely publicized designers. He maintained his subscription to *Domus*, which was increasingly publishing not only Italian work but also Scandinavian and American, and in its pages he followed the then-current work of Gunnar Asplund, Ralph Erskine, and Reima Pietilä. He also followed Carlo Scarpa's career, though less attentively, at a time when few outside Italy did so; he had seen Scarpa's Olivetti showroom in Venice on a side trip during the Stuttgart year. He continued to study, at occasional intervals, Robert Maillart's bridges and his few buildings. Above all, Lovett maintained his interest in Aalto. Aalto had completed his stunning church at Imatra in 1959, and from 1955 to 1969 was designing the campus of Otaniemi Technical University; its renowned Lecture Hall was finished in 1963. In the same year, Aalto began the design of his second American building, a library for Mount Angel Seminary in the hills near Salem, Oregon, not far from Seattle, that would be the finest of his several libraries. These influences, and Lovett's own development of the ideas and beliefs that shaped the Hilltop remodeling, would be the foundations of his subsequent work as it was to evolve over the next four decades.

3.1 Lovett, the
Lovetts' Crane Island
retreat, San Juan
Islands, 1970. Wasp
passage, and the
retreat, from the
beach.

The Crane Island Retreat

In 1970 Lovett began the little weekend retreat for himself and his family on Crane Island, one of the smallest of the San Juans, north of Washington's Olympic Peninsula. The island can be reached solely by private transport, and its only buildings are a few small vacation structures.

The Lovetts had acquired a south-facing waterfront property overlooking Wasp Passage. Lovett felt that its remoteness and undisturbed ecology made it a kind of sanctuary, demanding a minimal architectural presence on the land and a minimal architectural incision into the land. He thought a small building might be primarily supported by just two small piers at the edge of the bluff above the beach. On these piers he would poise two triangular trusses, twelve feet apart and seemingly inverted from their usual configuration, that would cantilever out over the bluff toward the water. The geometry of the trusses, the shapes and relationships of the members, the means of their connections, and the dramatic cantilever, would establish the visual vocabulary of the little retreat. Inland, an opaque-walled volume on a light anchoring foundation wall would serve as a visual and physical counterweight. For this inland volume, rough-sawn cedar is the finish material inside and out; the stain color was selected to emulate the bark of the madrona trees on the site, one of which grows through the cantilevered deck.

3.2 *Crane Island Retreat. The retreat at the edge of the forest. (© Christian Staub)*

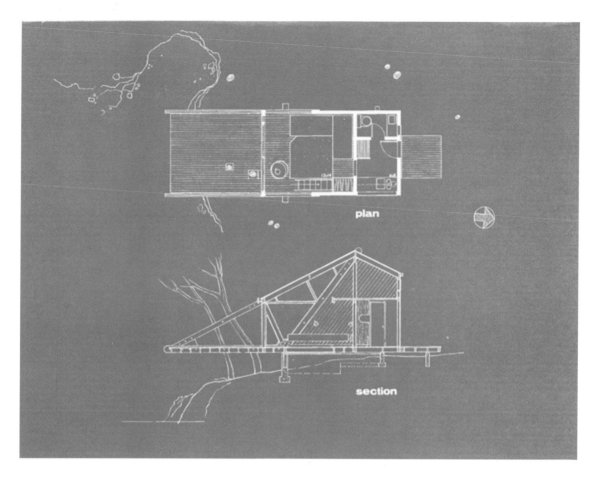

3.3 Crane Island retreat. Plan and section.

The site almost demanded a building that could be "produced as components and assembled with basic tools," as Lovett had intended the Hilltop house to be twenty years earlier. All elements of the Crane Island retreat were thus entirely prefabricated so that only assembly was required at the site. And they all had to be sized to allow transport by car and small private boat. The trusses, on which the formal and spatial organization, visual image, and structural stability depend, are built from simple mill-run pieces of vertical grain fir. All truss members were preshaped and predrilled for assembly at the site, by means of simple exposed bolted connections to companion pieces and to steel connecting plates. All bolts are modularly located. The top member of each truss, thirty feet long, is in fact made up of two fifteen-foot lengths joined at midpoint above the glazed south wall. The longest members are the eighteen-foot pieces with rounded ends that are the four identical lower sides of the trusses; these members, of course, determined the dimension of the cantilever over the beach.

The placement of the piers a few feet inland from the cornice of the bluff locates the retreat just at the edge of the wood, in part withdrawn into the trees and in part projecting from them. This was, perhaps, an obvious and inevitable location. Nevertheless, for Lovett it was also especially appropriate and meaningful. He had long been interested in Carl Jung's concept of a collective unconscious, including the suggestion that man might possess "an ingrained preference, inherited from man's primitive ancestors, for placing himself at the edge of the forest where he can look into the

3.4 Crane Island retreat. Looking north to the interior. Beyond the fireplace is the stair/ladder to the loft; the depressed floor is at center. (© Christian Staub)

3.5 Crane Island retreat. The interior looking south, from the cave behind the fire to the architectural meadow, and the prospect of land, sea, and sky. (© Christian Staub)

field from a secure vantage point."[1] Although this comment was the immediate endorsement of Lovett's intuition, the idea has a long history of literary and poetic expression, as Jung must have known. Of innumerable examples, one might cite a line from "The Marshes of Glynn," by the nineteenth-century American poet Sidney Lanier: "To the edge of the wood I am drawn, I am drawn."[2] And in more recent years Jung's observation, and Lanier's poem, have been corroborated by psychologists Stephen and Rachel Kaplan, whose empirical studies have shown that "neither being out in the open nor being in the woods is favored. The opposing vectors would tend to place the individual right at the forest edge. Ecologists point out that such an area is richest in terms of life forms; it is likely to be the safest as well."[3]

Thus Lovett's little retreat lies "right at the forest edge." To the north is dense foliage; to the south, a panoramic prospect of sea and sky. While the crisp geometry and the cantilevered deck sharply distinguish the little building from its natural surroundings, its experiential characteristics match those of the site. To the north, tucked within the firs and madronas, opaque surfaces enclose the bath, the kitchen, and the living space. On the west and north sides of the living space—within the wood— are upholstered foam seats that double as beds for two Lovetts. Forward of these, in the center of this living area, the floor plane is lowered, drawing the occupants closer to the earth, and making of the higher floor at the edges a containing boundary. A sleeping loft above the northern edge, for the other two

3.6 Crane Island retreat. From the west. (© Christian Staub)

Lovetts, creates a more intimate ceiling over the highest part of the living space; the loft is reached by the stair/ladder whose angle of ascent parallels the near truss chord. The "Toetoaster" fireplace, which Lovett had patented a few years earlier,[4] stands directly over the centerline of the piers, and so is appropriately just at "the edge of the wood." It marks the southern limit of the haven.

Beyond the fireplace, the deck extends the upper floor plane of the living space out into the sun. As one moves out onto the deck, both site and architecture open to sea and sky. The forest is left behind; the chord of the truss drops away; the platform hovers above the falling contours of the shore below; no protective rail intervenes to compromise the "vast sweet visage of space . . . where the gray beach glimmering runs."[5]

4.1 The west shore
of Whidbey Island at
the Miller site.

Lovett's Mature Career

In the same year, 1970, Lovett designed a small house for Prescott and Elizabeth Miller that is notable for its minimalist restraint. Mr. Miller was an engineer and Mrs. Miller had retained a serious interest in design from her student days at the Chicago Art Institute. They wished to build a small house for their approaching retirement years and would need only the usual domestic spaces plus a guest bedroom. They sought a house that would be clearly a man-made construct, a pure white form if possible, with both a sense of enclosure and an openness to the trees, the sea, and the sky. They had found a majestic site, a wooded bluff 200 feet above Puget Sound, on the west shore of Whidbey Island.

The Miller plan seems straightforward. Materials, too, are commonplace: the stucco exterior is simply detailed; interior walls are unbroken expanses of sheetrock. But the house is rich in subtleties. The master bedroom suite is isolated by two walls, a corridor, and two doors, at the Millers' request, to retain their privacy when guests are present. The hallway is graciously broad, almost an autonomous space. A degree of surprise is introduced by the angular elements of the plan, economically achieved by three short runs of angled wall, three roof edges, and the outlines of the entry walk and the western deck. The flat ceilings are organized to yield uncomplicated edge conditions, and are surfaced with Aalto-like cedar, while wood cabinet trim and wood bookcases bring warmth into the vertical plane. Space and light are manipulated by a north-facing clerestory at the eastern edge of the living space and by sloped ceilings over living and dining spaces. The clerestory is the most unusual of these devices. It gathers eastern light into the center of the house, and balances the illumination from the bright western windows, ensuring that people and objects are nowhere harshly silhouetted.

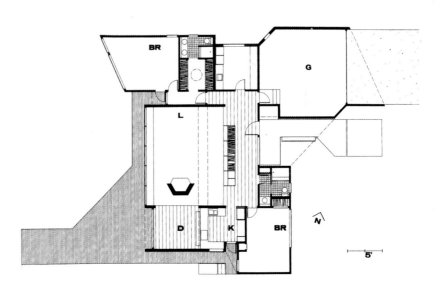

4.2 Lovett, the Prescott and Elizabeth Miller house, Whidbey Island, 1970. The entry court.

4.3 Miller house. Plan.

33

4.4 Miller house. The living room looking south toward the dining space; the light-balancing clerestory is at left.

4.5 Miller house. From the edge of the bluff, looking east.

Lovett had sensed in the Millers "a certain elegance and reserve," and he sought to create a setting appropriate to their imminent retirement, a place for a "restful and contemplative life."[1] His means were a studied simplicity, a perfection of proportion, the management of natural light, the limited but sophisticated use of wood, the oddly relaxing expansive breadth of the hallway, and a few subtle but correlated geometric surprises. On the most exciting and

dramatic site he would ever be offered, at the edge of its wood, he created for the Millers a home of peace and repose.

Lovett designed sixteen houses between 1972 and 1981, all of them in the Puget Sound area. The Max and Carol Scofield house of 1976 is representative. It is sited on a knoll of a steep wooded hillside on Mercer Island, a small island-city in Lake Washington, a few minutes' drive from downtown Seattle. Although flanked by houses to north and west, the Scofield site has a superb view south and east to Lake Washington.

Its configuration derives from an anthropomorphic analogy that informs many of Lovett's houses of that period. He notes that the human face, and the human front, convey information through their complex and flexible morphology, their sensory receptors, and their devices for gesture and expression; on the other hand, the human back is convex, inert, and uninforming. So too, the entry elevation of the Scofield house, its public side, is the anthropomorphic "back" of the figure. Opaque walls with convex curved corners suggest contained volumes beyond, but offer no other clues about those volumes. In another anthropomorphic gesture, however, a bridge with a tightly scaled projecting canopy reaches forward to offer shelter from weather, and invites entry.

One enters into a small foyer. At right is a half-hidden access to the master bedroom suite; ahead is a narrow skylit balcony terminating in a study whose balcony edge angles southward. The main living spaces, a story below, are reached by a convoluted path. Two 90 degree turns are needed to arrive at the stair, which in its descent turns through another 180 degrees; at the bottom one must again turn through 180 degrees to reach the living space by means of a narrow and low corridor, or must sidestep to the north to enter the sitting area, the cave. This path could

4.6 Lovett, the Max and Carol Scofield house, Mercer Island, 1976. The entry facade; the entry door is at left. (© Christian Staub)

easily have been elsewhere, and it could easily have been simpler. The configuration is deliberate. For as one moves from the entry onto the stair, one moves downward and outward, into a far more extensive space, and to a platform, the landing, that previews, from an elevated vantage point, at least a full hemisphere of the architectural material that lies beyond. One then turns one's back on this wealth of information, and moves down yet another level, into a relatively low and confined space from which one must rediscover, in an entirely different way, the architectural material previewed so differently a moment before. Within a quite small house, and in a small part of it, one has been led through an extraordinary sequence of spatial experiences.

At the foot of the stair one passes the cave, which is bounded by a curved exterior wall whose northern facet is skewed to the northeast. Lovett intends this wall to be, metaphorically, a cupping hand. The idea may

4.7 Scofield house. Plans.

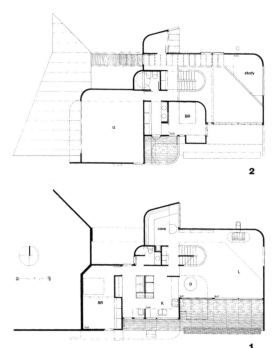

35

4.8 Scofield house. Isometric; the entry is at bottom center.

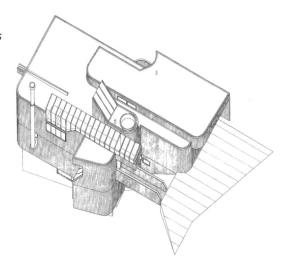

4.9 Scofield house. The interior, looking east from the vestibule.

be a manifestation of long-ago conversations with Gutbrod about the value of gesture as an informing concept; it may also owe something to Ralph Erskine's work, familiar to Lovett through *Domus* and through personal contact during the Stuttgart year. Lovett uses the configuration three times in the Scofield design: in the master bedroom; in the living space, as we will see; and in this sitting room. To engender a sense of containing reassurance, the hand bends around the space to hold it, and its occupants, against harm. The sitting room's built-in seating appropriately allies itself with—avails itself of—the embrace of this wall. The low ceiling, of Lovett's typical wood strips, reinforces the reassuring sense of containment; a window offers an appropriate view into dense vegetation along the north face of the house.

Between the stair and north wall of the house is the narrow book-lined corridor, with its own low wood ceiling. Its compression, created by the deliberate location of the stair volume, dramatizes the release of the more brightly lit living space beyond. The fireplace is on axis with this corridor, and so is the first thing seen as one moves into the living space. (The fireplace is one of several of Lovett's attempts to improve the thermal contribution of a design element that is usually largely symbolic. Steel tubes that serve as the hearth continue upward behind the fire, then bend forward to project into the room above the fire opening; they are meant to redirect into the room heat from fire and flue that would otherwise be lost.)

The low wood ceiling around the fireplace creates a second cave. This cave too, and the entire living space, from the north around to the east, are held by a second and far larger metaphoric hand, the curved wall that enfolds and protects. From the balcony edge southward, the living space is open to the roof; the interior meadow is flooded with light from the skylight above the balcony, and from the entirely glazed south wall, as the hand opens, releasing the space. Beyond, extending the floor plane, the deck reaches out over the hillside and commands a view southward the length of Lake Washington.[2]

The exterior of the Erling and Ila Larsen house of 1978 is equally an example of "back" and "face": it presents a mute facade to the street, while its west and south "faces" express the particular challenges of the site as they relate to the occupants within. The Larsen house occupies a rather bare hill-crown in a southern suburb of Seattle; the design must exploit magnificent views, while shielding habitable spaces from the sun and the unchecked southwest winds that beset the site. It is a tribute to the sculptural success of the house that, especially in views from the southwest, it makes its own case for this interpretation. In the interior the high-ceilinged, light-flooded living space opens to views of enormous reach to west and south. At the northwest corner of this meadow is the cave, the small low-ceilinged opaque-walled study with built-in seating. Above, the master bedroom is also treated as a place of refuge, with a low ceiling, an abundance of opaque walls, and a limited view to the northeast.

In recognition of the quality of these and many other similar residences, Lovett was elected to Fellowship in The American Institute of Architects in 1978.

By that date he had worked through many permutations of his stop and go spaces, his caves and meadows; he had learned to direct choices of materials to his purposes; to manage light, and darkness; to prolong and enrich experiential perceptions by means of distance and convolution. The house designed in 1981 for Gerhardt Morrison and Julie Weston illustrates those devices—or all but one—in a house of average size and modest budget, at a late point in Lovett's career. The

4.10 Scofield house. The sitting room and study at the foot of the stair, held against harm by an architectural hand.

4.11 Scofield house. The book-lined path, with the fireplace on axis ahead.

small lot in Seattle's Leschi neighborhood, above the west shore of Lake Washington, offers views to Mount Rainier and the Cascade Range, with Lake Washington in the foreground. The approach traverses a walled garden. Within, the stair lies ahead; the path to

the main floor space entails a swerve to the right, following the curved garage wall. The path is wide—Lovett calls it an interior "street"—and above it are two different ceiling planes. The left side is under a low ceiling and leads to the more intimate kitchen and dining spaces, while over the broader right side of the "street" the ceiling height is fully seventeen feet.

To the right a rectangular box rises through almost two stories, terminating in a glazed band just under the roof. Both Morrison and Weston are lawyers and this is their "law library." It is entered through a centered opening—a rare example of symmetry in Lovett's work—that is meant to emphasize the library's importance to the clients. It, and the other wall-defined spaces, were thought of as buildings along the "street," each formed according to its use and meaning. The gently curved wall of the kitchen nudges toward three steps that lead downward into the living space. The high ceiling continues above the fireplace, bringing light from an east-facing clerestory above. Over the remainder of the living space, however, the ceiling is at the lower plane, and the vertical dimension is greater than the dining space only by virtue of the lowered floor. The proportions direct attention toward the view, and the lower ceiling makes possible a splendid terrace for the master bedroom above, but the cave and meadow theme is less dramatic here than in most of Lovett's late work. Interior surfaces are of simple painted gypsum wallboard, at the clients' request, as neutral display surfaces for their art collection. The luxuries here are space, light, and choreographed movement.

From 1987 onward Lovett was at work on the Villa Simonyi, introduced in the prologue; it is the subject of an independent chapter to follow. In 1993, when that project, already large, seemed likely to continue to grow through several phases of additions, Lovett was asked by David Cutler and Debrah Girdler to design a house for their site, also in Medina.

Lovett was then associated with a colleague, Charles J. Williams III, who had been in the graduate program in architecture at Washington in the mid-1980s, and thus was one of Lovett's last students before he retired from teaching in 1987. Though that side of his life has not been emphasized here, Lovett was

4.12 Scofield house. The living space; dining is to the left.

4.13 Scofield house. The southern elevation.

4.14 Lovett, the Erling and Ila Larsen house, Seattle, 1978. The exterior from the southwest.

4.15 Lovett, the
Gerhardt Morrison
and Julie Weston
house, Seattle, 1981
Plans.

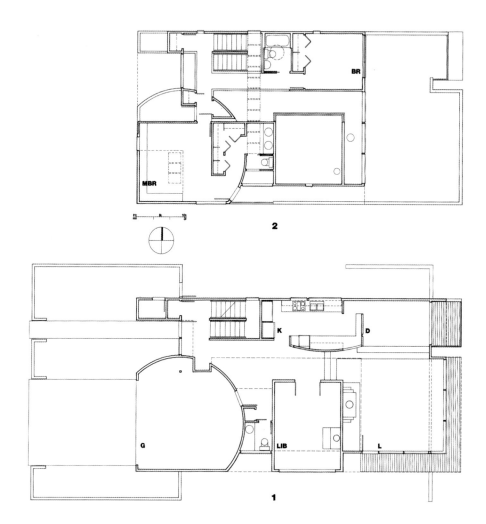

4.16 Morrison-
Weston house. The
law library. (©
Christian Staub)

4.17 Morrison-
Weston house. The
"street," looking west
from the living room
toward the entry; the
curved kitchen wall is
at right.

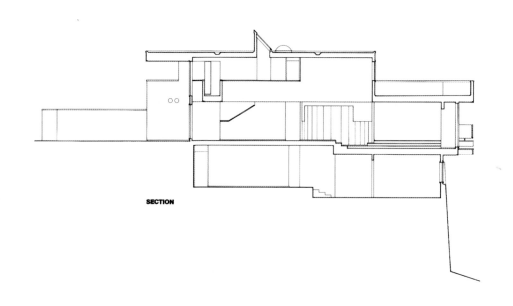

SECTION

an accomplished teacher; he taught in design studios, and the thoughts that informed his work were central to his teaching. Having been an instructor for several of Williams's design studios, Lovett was a member of Williams's thesis committee. The thesis became a superb proposal for a Cultural Center near Otaniemi, Finland, that built on the experiences of a year Williams had spent in Finland as a Valle scholar. In 1992 Lovett invited Williams to join him as an associate architect for the pending Simonyi additions.[3] With the arrival of the Cutler-Girdler project, Williams assumed the role of project architect, responsible for schematic options and resolution, design development, final design execution, and site supervision during the three years of construction. Lovett would bear final responsibility, and would serve as guide and critic throughout. Susana Covarrubias, who had come to Seattle from Santiago, Chile, was also then working

with Lovett, and had been for several years: she had assisted with the Villa Simonyi design and had drawn almost all of the construction drawings for that project, by hand, in ink on mylar. She would continue in that role for the Cutler-Girdler house.

The Cutler-Girdler property was challenging. It is 320 feet east-to-west, and west of the

4.18 Morrison-Weston house. The living space, looking toward the dining area. (© Christian Staub)

4.19 Lovett, with
Charles J. Williams III,
the David Cutler and
Debrah Girdler house,
Medina, 1993-96.
Site plan.

4.20 Cutler-Girdler
house. Plans.

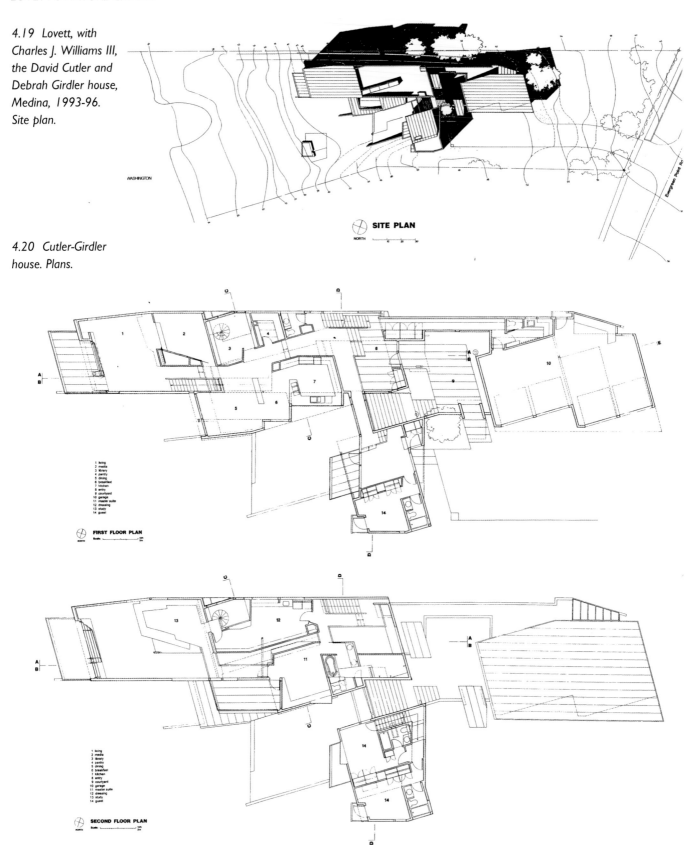

SITE PLAN

FIRST FLOOR PLAN

SECOND FLOOR PLAN

midpoint the south lot line angles southward about 15 degrees, to yield a shape not unlike an axhead. Shoreline laws forbid construction on most of the wider western part of the site, and the remainder has a breadth of only eighty feet. For this long and narrow slice of land, Cutler and Girdler required spaces whose total square footage is far in excess of the neighborhood's mandated minimum. Thus, among Lovett's houses, the Cutler-Girdler house is second in size only to the Villa Simonyi, but is compressed into a long footprint whose narrow dimension faces the street to the east and Lake Washington to the west.

Neighboring houses display their aspirations across manicured lawns, but the character and extent of the Cutler-Girdler house are masked until one passes through the entry gate and moves well into the site. Thus the house has no "back" or "front"; the site makes the issue moot. The driveway passes by a four-car garage (the clients are seriously involved in auto racing), whose facade, aligned with the 15 degree lot line deflection, is stepped to minimize its apparent breadth. From the drive the geometric themes of the house, and the palette of materials, are evident, revealing a richness and complexity unprecedented in Lovett's work.

In the Puget Sound area, southern and western elevations face severe weather. Those elevations are here clad in aluminum panels coordinated with the geometry of each elevation, and finished with a gray baked enamel. Other elevations are of stucco, contrasting with the metal panels in texture but coordinated in color. Lovett says the choice of materials was also "influenced by the regional marine, aircraft, and computer industries as well as the interests and active lifestyles of its owners," while "the form of the house is derived from the special nature of the site, the gently sloping land forms, and the actions of water, wind, and sun. The strongly

sheltering built volumes of the house itself take their cues, in addition, from the angles of the site as it opens to the beautiful expanse of Lake Washington to the west/southwest."[4]

From the western end of the drive a portal to the north leads to an entry courtyard. Within this, a broad stair at left leads downward to a garden and the shore; a bridge above connects the guest wing to the main

4.21 Cutler-Girdler house. The drive, looking west; the stepped facade of the garage is at right. (© Greg Krogstad)

4.22 Cutler-Girdler house. Looking north from the west end of the drive. (© Greg Krogstad)

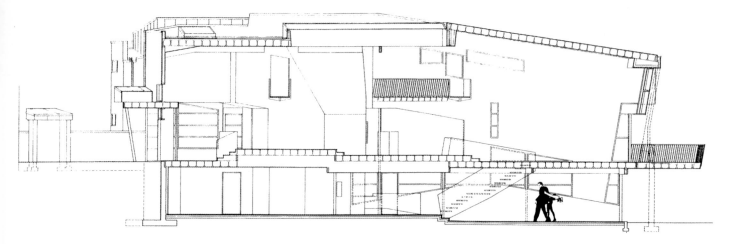

4.23 Cutler-Girdler house. East-west section through the "street." (Drawing by Susana Covarrubias and Slava Simontov)

4.24 Cutler-Girdler house. A "downspout." Water from the scupper falls on the titanium cylinder, thence down the cables to a like detail at grade. The "blinders" shield the walls from splashes.

the Morrison-Weston street are here developed in three dimensions. As seen from the vestibule, the Cutler-Girdler street deflects left, then right, and becomes brighter with distance, suggesting a trail that, disappearing around a bend, may lead to a sunlit clearing. "It is reminiscent for me," Lovett says, "of many many villages in Greece and Italy, and France and Germany, where you have always surprises along the way, and when you walk the street you can never see the full length."[6] This street rises through two stories to a skylight on the diagonal axis; steel bridges with maple rails link upper floor spaces across the void. To the left are the kitchen and the breakfast and dining spaces. At right are the stair to the upper floor, and a tiny powder room that plays with the nonorthogonal geometry. Beyond it to the west is a double-height library, with a high-tech version of the traditional library ladder at its upper level.

The hall narrows under the west end of the skylight, where a half-height wall separates the dining space from the hall, and screens a stair that leads down to the lakeside lawn and the shore. Directly ahead is a large brightly lit space with an extensive view. Immediately at right, however, a low opening leads to a low-ceilinged room, with continuous seating at right and ahead, whose only natural light comes through a minuscule east-facing win-

house. To the right of the stair and bridge is the entry.

Within is a generous vestibule, with a broad stair of four risers at right. At the top of this stair, directly ahead, is the hallway that is the spine of the house; Lovett has called this "a meandering, light filled 'street'";[5] it is the finest of his "go" spaces. The swerves and skews of

dow. This is the Cutler-Girdler cave; it is the purest and strongest example in all of Lovett's work. To the west it can be closed by sliding panels, or opened to the brightly lit two-story living space, two steps below, whose vistas extend across Lake Washington to the Seattle skyline, and south to and beyond Mercer Island. A deck extends the living space outward, above the lawn and the lakeshore.

The angular relationships of the Cutler-Girdler house, in two and even three axes, reiterate the geometry of the site, but they also recall the enveloping "hands" of the Hilltop remodeling, and the ideas weighed during Lovett's Stuttgart year. Many aspects of the house also suggest Lovett's empathy with Aalto's work, and Williams's recent encounters with that heritage: the 15 degree deflection of many elements, for example, is determined by the bend in the southern lot line, but it also echoes the deflection of the angular elements that characterize the Villa Mairea[7] and are repeated in many later examples of Aalto's work. The projecting windows on the south facade of the main block, and the west face of the guest wing, are intentional reinterpretations of a range of windows of the Villa Mairea. The faceted white surfaces of the Cutler-Girdler house shape a quality of space and light that evokes the more curvilinear interior of Aalto's church at Imatra, or, by means of a quite different geometry, the lecture hall at Otaniemi. Lovett has also acknowledged an interest in the work of both Frank Gehry and Daniel Liebeskind, from whom he found a greater freedom to be "wild and free" in this project. Charles Williams will have brought something of that dimension as well. His thesis project has a similar geometric character, and Lovett recalls of the house in its

4.25 Cutler-Girdler house. The powder room. (© Benjamin Benschneider)

4.26 Cutler-Girdler house. The "street," looking west from the upper level of the vestibule. (© Greg Krogstad)

4.27 Cutler-Girdler house. The "street"; the living space ahead, the cave to the right. (© Greg Krogstad)

4.28 Cutler-Girdler house. The library; from the upper floor.

4.29 Cutler-Girdler house. The cave, looking west to the architectural meadow.

early stages that "Charles developed some sections and I was tremendously excited. . . . I didn't really realize what we had until he built a small model of it."[8]

But Lovett's reflections on the Cutler-Girdler genesis are too modest. Of the above characteristics, only the windows derived from the Villa Mairea are simply "wild and free." The 15 degree deflections as they appear in two dimensions—in, for example, the powder room mirror, the jambs and sills of the living space fenestration, or the bridge and balcony rails—reiterate a controlled but complex geometric theme. Far from being merely "wild and free," they establish an order that pervades the design. But that order is manifested in more diverse and complex ways, and thus richer ways, than have appeared heretofore in

Lovett's work. The design, then, can be described as a visually apprehended complex order. In this context we might recall Lovett's early, and lifelong, passion for music, which can be described as audially apprehended complex order. As music is a complex order of sounds, the Cutler-Girdler house is a complex order of architectural material, and a remarkable example thereof. The old cliché that "architecture is frozen music" here finds a tangible illustration.

The angular deflections have an equally important spatial—and temporal—role. They are intrinsic to the richness of the vistas along the "street," and the vistas from the cave, the bridges, and the balcony above the living space. They are intrinsic even to the vistas from the living space to the lawn and the lake. Like the four-dimensional complex order of dance, these four-dimensional variations of vista lend

to the otherwise repetitive daily experiences of these spaces a quality of "endless discovery."[9]

Other characteristics of the Cutler-Girdler house derive from Lovett's beliefs—or, perhaps, those beliefs as he and an exceptional student, now colleague, have shared their development. Specifically, the scale and character of the spaces, and the manner of their interrelationships, reflect Lovett's deep inter-

4.30 Cutler-Girdler house. The meadow, looking east into the cave.

4.31 Cutler-Girdler house. The "street," looking east; the stair to the lower level is at right. (© Greg Krogstad)

4.32 Cutler-Girdler house. The meadow, looking southwest. (© Benjamin Benschneider)

est in human emotional responses to these matters—an interest that began in his pre-Stuttgart days—while the exuberant revelation of the way each part of the house is made is the extension of a childhood passion.

In 1993, the year in which Lovett began the Cutler-Girdler project, he was chosen to receive the AIA Seattle Medal, the highest honor the Seattle AIA can confer, awarded for distinguished lifetime achievement.[10]

*4.33 Cutler-Girdler
house. From the lake.
(© Greg Krogstad)*

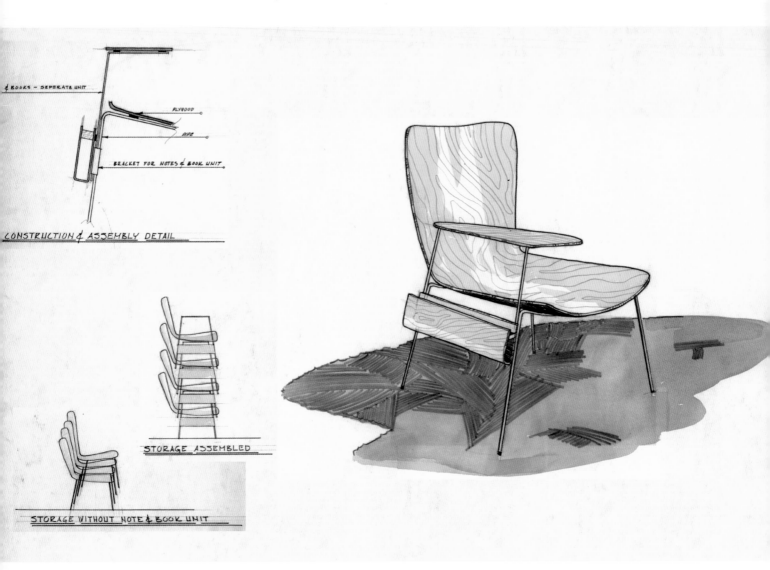

BOOKS – SEPERATE UNIT

PLYWOOD

PIPE

BRACKET FOR NOTES & BOOK UNIT

CONSTRUCTION & ASSEMBLY DETAIL

STORAGE ASSEMBLED

STORAGE WITHOUT NOTE & BOOK UNIT

5.1 Bystrom, a fourth year design studio sketch problem, 1951. (© University of Washington College of Architecture and Urban Planning Archives)

Arne Bystrom's Formative Years

Albin Bystrom came to Seattle from Sweden by way of Minnesota in 1914, working his way west as a logger. His considerable energy then led him north to Alaska, where he prospected, fished, built canneries, and met and married a Norwegian girl named Martha Hammerose. Albin and Martha came back to Seattle in about 1920, and made their home in the Ballard neighborhood.

They chose a city, and a neighborhood, intimately related to wood. Seventy years before the Bystroms arrived, the first nonindigenous settlers had come to what would be Seattle, and found themselves in the midst of the densest stands of timber on the North American continent. They quickly made timber the staple of their economy. By 1852, near what is now Seattle's Pioneer Square, Henry Yesler was milling lumber for booming San Francisco. A year later the Maine firm of Pope and Talbot crossed the continent to build a New England mill town—Port Gamble—on the Olympic Peninsula. When the railroads reached the northwest in the 1880s, other timber empires followed. By the early twentieth century much of Seattle's working population depended on wood for their livelihood, and this was especially true in the neighborhood the Bystroms chose for their home. The drying stacks of fir and cedar from Ballard's mills rose far above the cornices of its buildings, dominating the skyline. Its largely Scandinavian population included loggers, shingle weavers, shipwrights, and builders of the city's boardwalks and docks. Its craftsmen and carvers made furniture; its carpenters built Seattle's vast legacy of wooden buildings and the wooden forms that have yielded the extraordinary finish of local concrete work.

Carl Arne Bystrom, the last of Albin and Martha's four children, was born into that neighborhood on June 8, 1927. He remembers a close and supportive family life, and especially the many childhood evenings enlivened by stories of his father's adventures. By the time Arne was six he had made something of wood: he and his father, by then a longshoreman, made Arne's first pair of skis, from wood salvaged from a ship. The skis are evidence too of Arne's other love, the outdoor life that was encouraged by both the region's natural features and his admired father's experiences. Arne joined the local Boy Scout troop at the earliest possible moment. By the time he was thirteen he and Carsten Lien, a sixteen-year-old friend, had hiked—just the two of them—forty miles through wilderness to the Mount Deception trailhead. From there they climbed to the summit, the second highest in the Olympic Range. These were early foundations for later skills: in adult life Arne would be an expert skier and an accomplished mountaineer.

In grade school he was encouraged by his art teacher, though he remembers no particular art-related home experiences. In high school he did exceptionally well in math and physics, and he played varsity football. He entered the University of Washington in the spring term of 1945, and because of his strengths in math and physics he enrolled in aeronautical engineering; Boeing, builder of the B-17 and B-29 bombers for the war that was just ending, was a major local employer. But Arne found engineering unsatisfying. He stayed only through the spring quarter. He was called

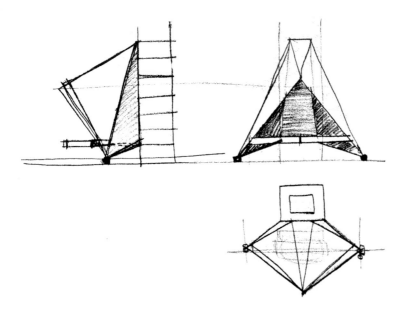

5.2 Bystrom, sketches for a metal fireplace, ca. 1958, intended for the Lien house but not executed.

into Army duty in September, and served with the occupation forces in Korea, "A time to think," he recalls.[1] His thinking led him to a decision: in December 1946, back in Seattle, he reenrolled at the University, in architecture, just in time for winter quarter of 1947.

In his first year he encountered the program in which Wendell Lovett was just completing his last two quarters. École des Beaux-Arts methods were still widespread. Lionel Pries was still the dominant figure, and he still imparted a rich cultural ambience and a catholic grasp of architectural sources including the emerging modernism. Arne remembers Pries's authoritative presence in studio and history classes, and he remembers, even more vividly, many evenings at Pries's home, in which Arne "was absorbed by" Pries's extensive architectural library.[2] But the school, like all others in those immediate postwar years, was entering a period of dramatic growth and, inevitably, significant change. In Arne's second year a few new teachers joined the faculty; in his third year these included Lovett, just back from MIT. Although modernism was by then represented by others at Washington, including Pries himself to some degree, Arne re-

members that Lovett conveyed its precepts exclusively, and with evangelistic fervor. Arne found in Lovett all of Pries's intense dedication and intellectual rigor, and the added dimension of a new idea.[3] So Arne was led through the world of Mies and Le Corbusier, Gropius and Breuer, and he remembers the excitement of that still-young movement. But he viewed pure European modernism with a skeptical eye. "Fortunately," he says, "we learned something about Alvar Aalto [through Lovett?] and Eero Saarinen, who were the 'humanizers' of the Bauhaus movement, which was pretty cold-blooded."[4] During these same school years, Arne and several classmates also actually built a small house, an experience that enlarged both his craft and construction skills and his under-standing of the role construction practices must play in design.

Arne also discovered Frank Lloyd Wright, and throughout his life that enthusiasm would remain as vivid as at his first encounter. (He is still quick to note that his birth date was Wright's sixtieth.) Wright's Unitarian church in Madison, Wisconsin, had been finished in 1947; dozens of his Usonian houses were completed, or in design or construction, in the late 1940s. Special issues of *Architectural Forum* dedicated to his work appeared in 1948 and 1950. But Wright lay outside both the École tradition and European modernism, and was quick to ridicule both, while his vast scope of work refused, and still refuses, easy formulation. For these and no doubt other reasons, Wright was only occasionally discussed in architectural schools at the time; in fact, he was largely ignored in academia until long after his death. (Nor did he fare much better in professional recognition.[5] Though he is now widely acknowledged as the most important American architect of the twentieth century, the American Institute of Architects awarded him its Gold Medal only in 1949.) Books on Wright also were few in number in Arne's college years. But in 1942

Henry-Russell Hitchcock had published *In the Nature of Materials* as an illustrated compendium of Wright's work, and for those who wished to ponder Wright's ideas and beliefs, his own flawed but intoxicating unillustrated *Autobiography* appeared in a heavily revised second edition in the following year. Arne discovered Wright through these books and through serials such as the special *Forum* issues. He still speaks of Wright's "total commitment to the site and the land, the relation between indoors and outdoors, as well as the use of natural materials. He loved stone for its own sake, and natural wood, and he was a master of space—of space, materials, and light."[6]

Arne graduated, summa cum laude, in 1951. Like Lovett before him, he was the AIA Silver Medalist.

After graduation he worked as a steel detailer with Seidelhuber Iron and Bronze Works, where in 1952, coincidentally, he fabricated the prototype of Lovett's "Firehood" metal fireplace. Arne stayed there for two years. The job paid well, and he wanted to save for a trip to Europe, to visit the buildings he, like most of his contemporaries, knew only from the drawings and black-and-white photographs in Banister Fletcher's ubiquitous history text,[7] and the black-and-white lantern slides in the history classes. Arne wanted to see the great buildings for himself, and, having begun a serious interest in photography, he wanted to photograph them all in color.

By 1953 he had enough money to fund himself and his boyhood friend Carsten Lien; together they would do a four-month Grand Tour. (The term originates in the formulaic tour of European monuments that, for those who could afford it, would complement an École des Beaux-Arts education. Such "tours," with, usually, a revised selection of sites, are now commonplace among architectural students, and most architectural schools—indeed, most college programs—offer many foreign study opportunities. But at that date, with Arne's resources and expectations, such an opportunity might never recur.) Students and recent graduates of Washington's architecture program who planned an extended trip to Europe traditionally turned to Lionel Pries for guidance, and Arne did so. Although Pries had been to France and Italy only once, during his own year-long tour of Europe in 1922-23, he had taught their architecture for twenty-five years, and he helped Arne to shape an itinerary heavily slanted toward those countries.[8] Arne and Carsten, itinerary in hand, booked passage on an austere utilitarian transport ship, and landed in Le Havre; they immediately headed south. Carsten had the impression that Arne was primarily interested in the architecture of Renaissance Italy, and they bicycled and hitchhiked to Venice, Florence, and Rome.[9] These were sites central to the École philosophy. Pries had visited them at length on his own long-ago tour and had found them indelibly valuable; it is fair to attribute to him their inclusion in Arne's and Carsten's plans.

Then, while Carsten stayed in Italy to study Renaissance music, Arne went north, to France. Pries, in France on that one occasion decades earlier, had been to Strasbourg, Angoulême, Carcassonne, Albi, and Paris, and the tiny village of Longpont near Soissons. With one exception, these were not the destinations Arne was seeking. He pursued an itinerary that must have been largely his own. Traveling by train, by bicycle, and on foot, visiting, alone, sites far less crowded then than now, he seems to have satisfied his own tastes, perhaps discovering within them a more intense dimension of which he was himself only dimly aware. The AIA Silver Medal he had been awarded at graduation was always accompanied by a copy of Henry Adams's classic *Mont-Saint-Michel and Chartres*, and Arne

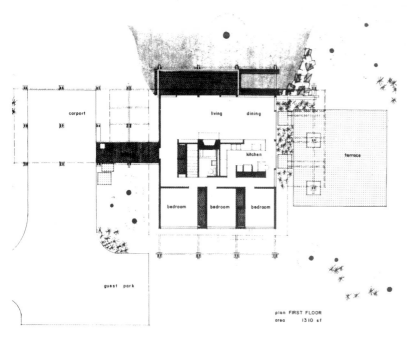

had read it, cover to cover.[10] He now discovered at firsthand the ambience and the buildings from which Adams had drawn his prose. Fifty years later Arne's most vivid memories of the trip—and they are very vivid indeed—are of lingering days at the great French medieval sites, and especially Albi, Amiens, Saint-Denis, Mont-Saint-Michel, and Chartres. He still speaks of them excitedly, and with transparent affection.

In contrast, on his return to Seattle he took a position with Paul Thiry, one of Seattle's earliest practitioners of European modernism.[11] Arne worked on several projects during his four years of employment there, although his own later work would have little in common with Thiry's spare International Style. "As a young architect at that time, you

5.3 *Bystrom and Greco, the Carsten Lien house, Seattle, 1958; first floor plan.*

5.4 *Lien house. The exterior. (© Art Hupy, courtesy of University of Washington Northwest Collection)*

5.5 Lien house. The interior: the living room. (© Art Hupy, courtesy of University of Washington Northwest Collection)

wanted to work for either Paul Thiry or Paul Kirk. Thiry did not go as much into wood expression as Kirk did, but he was a more profound architect . . . probably the most important architect of this region at that time. It was not a very big office, six or seven working there. He let me design a lot."[12] In the same years Arne also made pilgrimages to Wright's Johnson's Wax Building in Racine, Wisconsin, and "Fallingwater" in southwest Pennsylvania.

In 1958 he was asked to design a house for Carsten Lien and his family. He gambled that the fee, and perhaps the publicity if the project went well, might be enough to support the beginnings of an independent practice. He asked fellow Thiry employee James Greco, a superb architectural draftsman and detailer, to join him in an architectural partnership. The firm practiced as Bystrom and Greco until 1967.

Bystrom and Greco's Lien house, like Lovett's earliest work, is transparently Miesian. Lien recalls that "Arne was so intent on purity of design that he refused to accept that we had to have a stairway from the main floor to the lower level." Given Bystrom's affection for Wright and for the medieval buildings of Europe, his Scandinavian background, his skepticism about European modernism, and his eagerness to know the work of Aalto and the Saarinens, this may be surprising. But several influences were guiding Bystrom's work, then and for some time thereafter. Lien believes it would not have occurred to Bystrom at the time to express anything Scandinavian, as such

5.6 Paul Hayden Kirk, Blair Kirk house, Seattle, 1951. The exterior. (© University of Washington Libraries, Special Collections, the Dearborn-Masser Collection, DM2363)

a background was the subject of jokes; one wanted to be "just an American." More important, the Miesian mode, already mentioned for its influence on Lovett's earliest work, was genuinely pervasive, evident even in the younger Saarinen's contemporaneous General Motors Technical Center. The other influence shaping Bystrom's work was Lovett himself; Bystrom recalls that "Wendell's aura guided my decisions for years."[13]

Nevertheless, the Lien house is a Miesian exercise in wood, and this quality is assertive. It represents Bystrom's personal affection for the material; it also draws from the work of earlier and contemporaneous architects in the region who approached the material with equal dedication. Of these, Bystrom has mentioned Paul Hayden Kirk. Kirk (1914-95) was a 1937 graduate of Washington who by the mid-1950s had evolved a personal style and

a national reputation.[14] Although his work was in many ways Miesian, he incorporated a catholicity of influence that may well have had its origins in Pries's teaching. Kirk's style exploited the "bypass" connections typical of earlier buildings in both Scandinavia and Japan, in which vertical and horizontal wooden members are joined side by side; each, bypassing the other, projects expressively beyond the intersection. (Such a connection is not necessarily structurally straightforward; a beam joined to a column in this way, for example, cannot transfer load by direct bearing but must do so by means of an inherently less efficient shear connection. But the bypass concept has precedent in the work of Mies himself, at the steel-framed Farnsworth house in Plano, Illinois of 1955, for example. Used in wood construction, the aesthetic attraction of the bypass connection is that it yields, in almost decorative degree, an expressive articulation of each member of the material fabric.) Kirk also managed to use remarkably slender and delicate wood members for structure, trim, and ornamentation, lending an oriental delicacy to his work. He used clapboard, shiplap, and cedar shingle siding for crisply tailored expanses of wall, and the resulting tension between a romantic texture and a crisply modernist geometry is a hallmark of his work. In materials, proportions, and connective devices—the ubiquitous bypass detail is one example—Bystrom's Lien house reveals a considerable debt to Kirk, and probably to others as well.

The Lien house was published in the *Pacific Architect and Builder*, and was the *Seattle Times/ AIA Seattle* "Home of the Year." The recognition brought to the firm, in the following year, houses for Michael Adams, Frank Anderson, and F. Deckebach, an addition to the Howard Miller house, an Elks Club remodeling, and commissions for the H. P. White Apartments, the Robertson Clinic, the Sand Point Country

5.7 Bystrom and Greco, the firm's new office on Bellevue Avenue in Seattle, 1963. The exterior.

5.8 Bystrom and Greco, the new office. The interior.

Club, and a cafe for restaurateur Stuart Anderson. In 1960 the firm did three more houses, for Tordal Dannevig, Robert Zech, and Bystrom's father Albin. The Bystrom and Zech houses received AIA Seattle "Home of the Month" awards, while the Zech and Miller projects, both of them similar to the Lien house, won major awards from *Sunset* magazine, and the Zech house was published in the prestigious *Interiors* magazine.

With some reason for confidence in the future, Bystrom married Valerie Broze on September 10, 1960. Daughter Ashley arrived in 1962, son Carl in 1965.

From 1960 to 1963 the firm designed several smaller private homes, two apartment buildings, and a second restaurant for Stuart Anderson. Many of these projects also received awards. In 1963 Bystrom and Greco remodeled a small 1930s commercial building on Capitol Hill to provide a more efficient and impressive office for their thriving practice. Its exterior testifies to the influence of Paul Kirk, and its interior to the continuing influence of

5.9 Bystrom and Greco, the Century Building, Seattle, 1963. The exterior. (© University of Washington Libraries, Special Collections)

Lovett's original Hilltop house.

In that same year the firm designed a brick-and-concrete office building—the Century Building—at the foot of Seattle's Queen Anne Hill. When it was completed in 1964, it was published in the *AIA Journal*, *Progressive Architecture*, and *Architecture West*, and it received an award from the Prestressed Concrete Institute, the first national award for Bystrom or the firm. The Century Building was no longer either Miesian or Lovettian. It is contemporaneous with Lovett's completion of the Hilltop remodel, and Bystrom, like Lovett, would have been aware of the many architects who were then attempting to enlarge, or free themselves from, the modernist canon. Of these, Bystrom and Greco were clearly influenced by Paul Rudolph's work just prior to the Yale project, and especially his high school for Sarasota, Florida, of 1958-59. The Century Building was also influenced to a lesser extent, perhaps, by Louis Kahn's Richards Laboratories, while the massing—a main body of office space, an entry link to the right, and then a separate elevator mass—is clearly indebted to Wright's Larkin Building in Buffalo, New York of 1902. But unlike Lovett's Hilltop remodeling, which was the point of departure for all of his work to follow, the Century Building would be without issue. The firm moved their offices into the building shortly after it opened, but neither Bystrom and Greco nor Bystrom practicing alone would ever do anything quite like it again.

The next three years of the Bystrom and Greco practice included two houses in Seattle, one in Bellevue, and an alteration project for the University. In 1967 Greco left the firm. In 1968, as a consequence of the two earlier projects for Stuart Anderson, Bystrom, practicing alone, was designing four prototypical restaurants—two in Seattle, one in Bellevue, one in Tacoma—for Anderson's "Black Angus" chain. Anderson sought a rustic

western steakhouse image, so a Miesian ambience was out of the question from the outset, and for the same reason there was not much one could draw from Corbu, Saarinen, Rudolph, Kahn, Kirk, or Yamasaki. For this project Bystrom had to find his own direction, and it would owe very little to any outside influence. He began with the discipline of a structural system, as a Miesian adept in physics and math might do. But the system he developed was itself thoroughly un-Miesian. Hefty peeled logs[15] would serve as columns to support oversized rough-sawn wood beams and joists, with floors and ceilings of wood

5.10 Bystrom, "Black Angus," San Mateo, California, 1971. The exterior.

5.11 "Black Angus," San Mateo. The interior.

59

5.12 Bystrom, Madrona Dance Studio, Madrona neighborhood, Seattle, 1968. The exterior.

5.13 Madrona Dance Studio. The interior.

planks, all of this exposed to view on the interior. Quite aside from its western steakhouse mood, however, this system gave Bystrom a flexibility that modernism had so often sought, and one useful for a prototypical design. For it left the complementary rough-sawn wooden walls and floors free of any structural duties, so they could follow different plan dispositions as dictated by site conditions. Bystrom did two more restaurants for the chain in 1971, and two more in 1973. Several of these buildings still remain; their ambience is one of sophisticated rusticity.

In the same late 1960s, when the "Black Angus" work was under way, Bystrom was commissioned to design adaptive remodelings of the public bathhouses at Seward Park, Greenlake, and Madrona, as the first projects of Seattle's Forward Thrust Program of urban amenities. The existing bathhouses were brick structures, unspectacular but handsome

5.14 Bystrom,
Seward Park Cultural
Arts Center, Seward
Park, Seattle, 1968.
The exterior.

professional designs of the 1930s; those at Green Lake and Seward Park benefit from choice settings within elements of the Olmsted Brothers' Seattle Park System of 1903-31. The adaptations were to accommodate radical changes of usage: Seward Park was to be a Cultural Arts Center, Greenlake a Theater, and Madrona a Dance Studio. These adaptations required considerable interior remodeling, and the resultant interiors are clearly indebted to the "Black Angus" concept. The exteriors accept as a base the existing brick walls. Above these, the Madrona and Seward Park projects entailed higher superstructures. These are shingle-clad forms of crisp yet imaginative geometry, whose seemingly straightforward artlessness clothes a considerable formal stature.

With these projects of the late 1960s Bystrom moved away from the formal vocabulary of canonical European modernism, and set Lovett's influence aside as well. Yet only in the Century Building did he try to assimilate any of the new directions being marked out by the heavily publicized figures of the time. More surprisingly, except for the massing of the Century Building, there is no evidence of Bystrom's enduring admiration for Wright. In the "Black Angus" projects and the bathhouses, still working within the methodological precepts of modernism, Bystrom found a way to evolve a formal vocabulary of his own, and one intimately associated with his affection for wood.

6.1 Bystrom, The Bystrom's Raft River retreat on the Washington Coast, 1970-1978. The approach through the woods.

The Raft River Retreat

The Quinault Reservation on the Washington coast is, in fact, a fee-simple grant to several tribes, who from time to time have sold parcels of the land. In the early 1960s mountaineer Jim Whittaker acquired such a parcel, a remote tract sixty miles from a sizable town, with 1300 feet of Pacific shoreline. Bystrom often hiked and climbed with Whittaker, and on one such outing in 1964 Bystrom negotiated the purchase of 100 feet of dramatic ocean frontage within the tract, near the Raft River. The Bystroms tented there on summer weekends until 1970, when they decided to build a permanent shelter. They began construction themselves in 1971. Bystrom had continued into his adult life his early habit of making things from wood; he would always have in his house a professionally complete shop. The Raft River project was well within his skills and those he had led his family to learn. But all work was done with hand tools, and at a singularly remote site, so the work went slowly, and the considerable interior cabinetwork and furnishings were not complete until about 1978.

The Bystroms agreed that no major tree would be cut down. The cabin would be "fitted into and among the trees . . . the site merging with the residence," hence the eighteen-by-eighteen-foot plan dimensions, with corners oriented toward the cardinal points. A height of eighteen feet could provide two usable floors; the cabin would be a cube. It could rest on a few cylindrical piers, with no regrading for a slab, and no excavation for foundation

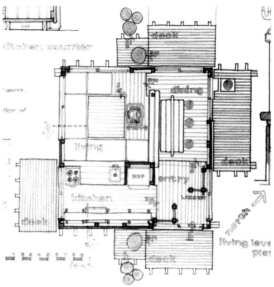

6.2 *Raft River retreat. The site and roof plan and plans of the upper and lower levels.*

63

*6.3 Raft River
retreat. Sections.*

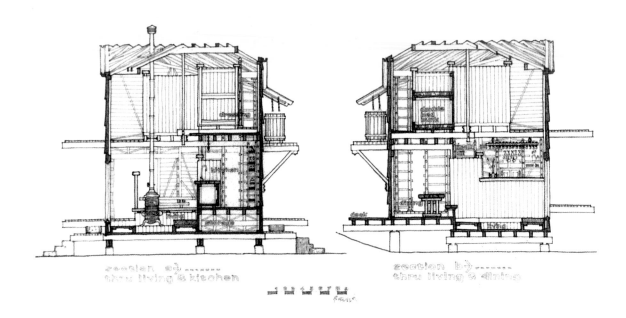

*6.4 Raft River retreat.
Sketches and studies
of "furnishings."*

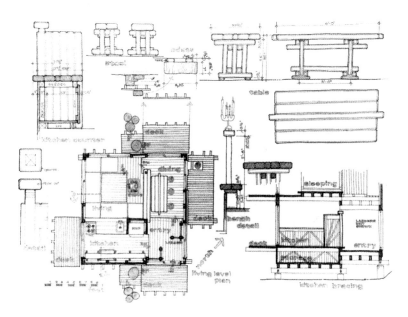

walls. The site would be all but undisturbed.

Yet the Bystroms had disliked the confusion of tent life, and the new cabin, though small, must provide a specific space for each activity. Bystrom says of its spatial composition, and here again one hears the canons of modernism: "The plan is a study in the minimum space needed for each human activity. How big is the optimum conversation group? Ten by ten feet. How much space is needed for dining? Seven by ten feet.'" Thus the main floor includes spaces for living and for dining, each at the above size, and an entry and a kitchen; each of these spaces is defined by changes in floor level and by built-in cabinetwork and furnishings. The composition is roughly symmetrical around the east-west diagonal. Above, also symmetrical about the east-west diagonal, and reached by two ladders in the entry, are two double bunk-bed cells, with a deck projecting from each.

The physical elements of the little cabin also reveal a modernist's predilection for the systematic, even the prototypical. Many drawings Bystrom made for the cabin show subassemblies drawn at large scale, then each part of the subassembly is drawn individually, and the required quantity specified. The entry ladders, for example, are drawn at 1/2" = 1', then the parts are individually drawn as an illustrated list titled, logically enough, "Parts." Listed, and drawn, are "1-3/4" Phillips head [screws]—240 req'd"; "1-5/16" Closet pole 2'–2-1/4"—30 req'd [for rungs]"; and seven other typical part types that, assembled, will make the two ladders. Stock factory-produced sliding glass door units open the lower exterior walls of the cabin's living space; similar units open the kitchen and the dining spaces to their respective decks, and each sleeping loft to its deck. Two such sliding units enclose the entry. There is here, in a sense, design by means of an organization of fabricated elements that in another context could describe a factory-manufactured dwelling. We are reminded of Lovett's contemporaneous Crane Island retreat, and still more of his first Hilltop house, designed during Bystrom's next-to-last year in school, when Lovett "was always thinking, at this time, of things that could be produced as components and assembled with

basic tools."[1] But similar intentions could hardly yield more different outcomes.

Opaque wall surfaces are clad with shakes over horizontal fir board sheathing. This cladding contributes very little lateral stiffness, and at the lower level the areas of opaque wall are relatively narrow. The site is in earthquake country, and the winds from the Pacific batter the coast. Lateral stiffness is therefore essential, and, given the vocabulary of the structure, it must be provided by the small areas of opaque wall. Bystrom has provided each such area with interior diagonal bracing, which, since there is no interior finish surface, is evident to the eye, as an "expression of the natural forces—the stresses—and their resolution."[2] At first glance the diagonals

6.5 *Raft River retreat. A study model of the structural system.*

6.6 *Raft River retreat. The exterior from the north.*

6.7 Raft River retreat. The exterior from the northeast.

6.8 Raft River retreat. The interior of the entry, with ladders to lofts.

6.9 Raft River retreat. The interior, from the north corner looking south.

6.10 Raft River retreat. Looking up to the skylight roof.

appear to follow a haphazard geometry that seems artlessly appropriate to the casual purposes of the building. A closer look reveals a studied system of impressive efficiency: every panel is triangulated without exception, and all triangulations tie to key points of strength within the geometry. This is a physicist's rusticity.

The four-foot cedar barn shakes, in their texture, and in their coloration as they weather, associate the exterior with the forest all around, while the glazed sliding doors, and the rail-less decks, draw the interior spaces out into the trees. But the forest is one of dense conifers; only a transparent roof could hope to bring in abundant light. Bystrom divided it into a series of triangular panels sloping to north and south from a diagonal ridge beam that connects the east and west corners of the cabin; these smaller members produce a horizontal truss whose geometry yields an unusually strong roof structure. The roof is further strengthened by short diagonal beams across east and west corners, and by a central post bolted to projecting beams of the upper floor system.

Thus the methodology behind the little cabin's design is purely modernist. Its material entity likewise owes little to subsequent philosophies: there is no evidence in it of Venturi's *Complexity and Contradiction*,[3] none of the references to historic typology or detail that by the early 1970s were ubiquitous to Postmodernism. The most avant-garde influence is seen, perhaps, in the light wood frame and the crisply geometrical shingled surfaces that might owe something to Kirk; but Kirk's influence was available from the mid-1950s. Yet the mood is neither pure modernism nor Kirk's modernism. The meticulous and rigorous plan, the seemingly casual structural sophistication, the deceptively artless big barn shakes, and the wealth of interior architectural material, indicate Bystrom's growing comfort with his own kind of modernism.

There is no water service, and the Bystroms decided not to drive a well. Washing water is drawn from the barrel that rests on the cantilevered platform at loft level above the entry; it collects rainwater from the east slope of the roof. Drinking and cooking water is packed in. Calls of nature are answered by a separate privy to the north.

Bystrom's little retreat, like Lovett's, is at "the edge of the wood." It is also at the edge of the continent, and it claims its "vast sweet visage of space" from a dramatically elevated vantage point. Ladders, to be climbed with effort and care, lead to the more perilously elevated sleeping lofts. The lofts have only minimal railings where they overlook interior living spaces below, and no railings at all on their wooden decks that wander out toward

6.11 Raft River retreat. The edge of the continent, and the Pacific surf.

the edge of the earth, dramatizing—augmenting, in fact—the dangers of the setting. The description of these little sleeping places immediately conveys a sense of thrill. Paradoxically, the word combines both fear and pleasure, and we do not necessarily associate that with sleep. Yet anyone can sense the delight of a night spent sleeping in one of these lofts, or perhaps more accurately the delight of lying awake in one of them, among the branches, with the nearby roar of the surf, as night falls. The emotion can be imagined in only slightly lesser degree in any of the little retreat's spaces. For in dramatizing the perils of its setting, the little architectural haven also dramatizes its own reassurance, as it echoes and merges with the forest, our more ancient haven.

In 1979 the little shelter received from the American Institute of Architects a National Honor Award, the most prestigious of the profession's commendations for an individual building. It may be the smallest building ever to have been so honored. The Institute's jurors described it as "a box filled with light by the sea . . . , a cabin Thoreau would have loved."

7.1 Bystrom, the new
Bystrom office in the
Pike Place Market,
Seattle, 1974.

Bystrom's Mature Career

During the years from 1970 to 1978, while Bystrom was designing and building the little Raft River retreat, he played a major role in the rehabilitation of Seattle's Pike Place Market. He was on the Market's Board of Directors, and served as architect for the Soames-Dunn Building rehabilitation, the Seattle Garden Center, and Sur La Table, a kitchenwares shop. The latter project included the design, in 1974, of a second floor to house a new office for Bystrom's practice. He did much of the construction of the office himself, and had the drafting desks built by Evert Sodergren, a Seattle furniture craftsman whose skills Bystrom would rely on for the later Dennis commission. Bystrom also continued his work for Stuart Anderson's "Black Angus" restaurant chain and he embarked on a series of residential projects that share a spatial and structural theme.

The first of these was for Peggi Moore. She came to Bystrom in 1977 seeking a residence that would include the usual domestic spaces plus a guest room for children and friends, and a studio over a two-car garage. She had seen several of the "Black Angus" buildings, and she seems to have wanted something of their character. Bystrom remembers that "she wanted a house of heavy timbers with a bedroom loft, a pitched roof, and high spaces. To her that represented the essence and spirit of the country."[1]

Bystrom had used log columns in the "Black Angus" buildings, and in doing so he had spent quite a lot of time studying vernacular pole structures. In contemplating the Moore project, he now considered analogies to a more sophisticated tradition of columnar wood construction: he made a series of sketches, some abstract, some analytical, of the eleventh- and twelfth-century stave churches of his ancestral Norway.

The several remaining examples of these churches are stepped pyramidal volumes with ascending tiers of steep shingled roofs; the wall surfaces are shingled, or of vertical boards, or boards and battens, or all three, and typically are without windows. The interiors, dimly lit from a single entry door, are dominated by heavy cylindrical wooden columns that determine a square, or nearly square, central space, and a surrounding ambulatory. Somewhat above eye level, wooden spandrels, whose curved undersides suggest arches, brace the columns to a band of horizontal ties. Immediately above is a continuous range of ornamented wooden x-bracing surmounted by a second band of horizontal members, with further knee-bracing above. Beyond, far

7.2 *New Bystrom office.*

71

7.3 Fantoft Stave Church, 13c. The exterior.

overhead, the upper reaches of the structure fade into the darkness of the roof's receding volumes.

For Bystrom's purposes, some aspects of this image would be more useful than others. The dark interior of the stave church creates an appropriately mysterious otherworld ambience that might well intensify religious emotion among the snow-laden conifers of a Norwegian hillside. But darkness is unlikely to appeal equally in a Pacific Northwest home, and an absence of windows would completely foreclose the integration of interior and

7.4 Hoprekstad Stave Church, 13c. The interior.

exterior that was one of Bystrom's central purposes. Nor does the typical stave church utilize Bystrom's familiar bypass connections; the axes of columns, horizontal ties, and bracing are always co-planar. On the other hand, the stave-church image is usefully elastic in scale, since the dimensions of actual examples vary widely. The cylindrical columns and the redundant bracing give the wooden structure a palpable sculptural presence and an appealing sense of formidable strength. And there is the seminal suggestion that such a robust assemblage of timber—not unlike that of the "Black Angus" buildings—is most appropriately clad in light shingled surfaces, like those of the Raft River retreat or the Seattle bathhouses, but built as an envelope external to the columnar structure. Bystrom was drawn to the idea of a clear articulation of skin and structure, and the inherent tension of contrast between the two, in visual, and actual, weight. And he found an emotional satisfaction

in the promise of durability, for the stave churches themselves demonstrate that such a wooden structure, shielded against the effects of time by independent and replaceable walls and roof, will last a millennium.

That Bystrom's adoption of the image would be convincing, however, is in large measure a consequence of the settings in which he would build. Few architects have enjoyed a sequence of sites as dramatic as those that would come his way, and for him they may have been especially inspiring because they epitomize the characteristics of the Puget Sound region that have been important to his life from childhood. There is also the happy coincidence that many of the sites his clients offered were remarkably Scandinavian in topography and vegetation. There is no better example than Peggi Moore's—thirteen heavily forested acres on Whidbey Island's western coast, at the edge of a majestic cliff, with Puget Sound's Admiralty Inlet below and the Olympic Mountains on the horizon. The grandeur of the site was matched by Moore's dedication to it. Bystrom says, "the woodland acres held for her a deep sentimental attachment."[2]

The house is approached by a curving path that meanders through trees of impressive dimension. Seen within them, the house is large; the simple repetitive geometries of its surfaces, and the absence of shadow-casting relief, make it seem larger still. Expanses of glass on delicate steel armatures rise into the peaks of the gabled facades, and so reveal a sturdy wooden armature within. The obviously rigid timber frame frees the exterior walls and roof from any structural role. They must carry only their own weight, and so, like those of the stave church, they are treated as a thin shingled skin lying outside the structural framework. Glazing is nearly co-planar with the shingles; roof meets wall without overhang or trim.[3] A bite taken out of the Moore facade at lower right creates a modest sheltering

7.5 Diagrammatic perspective of a typical stave church. (Drawing by T. William Booth.)

recess for the front door, through which one enters the interior.

Twenty-four log columns, each more than a foot in diameter, rise from the stone-paved floor to carry the partial upper floor and the roof far above. Sixteen of these columns mark out the grid of nine rectangles of varying dimensions that determines and controls the plan of the house proper. Six of the remaining eight columns define pavilions to north and south. The remaining two carry loads from atypical framing points, specifically the upper stair landing and the roof of the breezeway connecting house to garage. (The garage itself is of conventional stud-and-joist framing.) The upper floor is supported by joists above pairs of beams that bypass the columns on either

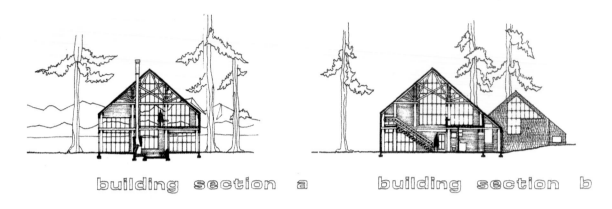

building section a   building section b

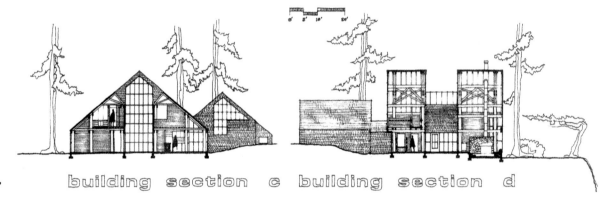

7.6 Bystrom, the
Peggi Moore house,
Whidbey Island,
1977. Plans and
sections.

building section c building section d

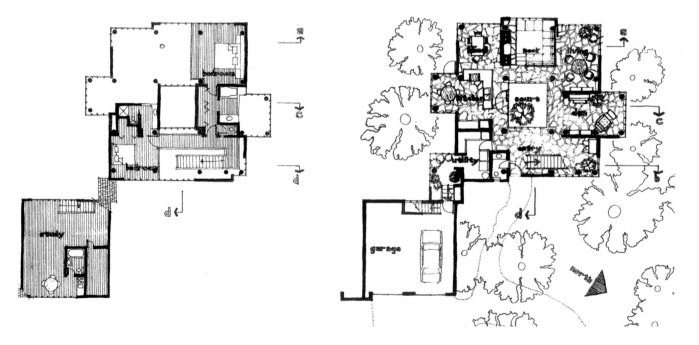

7.7 Moore house. The approach from the north.

7.8 Moore house. The nook, looking toward the glazed courtyard, with the kitchen beyond, at center.

side; a similar system supports the roof rafters and cross ties. The fans of diagonal bracing in both north-south and east-west axes, high in the roof's upper reaches, further stiffen the structure, and reiterate the stave-church image. But they do not live in stave-church darkness. Light is distributed throughout the core of the house by the glazed central void that, Bystrom says, "by introducing light and air to the center, creates a desired ambiguity between the sheltered inside and the forest outside. The resultant shaft of light is reminiscent of an opening in the forest canopy."[4]

Activities are accommodated by architectural material whose disposition seems casual but is in every case meticulously considered. The main floor drops a few risers into the nook just at the point where one most wants the earth at one's elbow. The dimensions of the nook, repeating those of the Raft River living space, are just right for conversation; the distance from the fire is just right for meditation. A low ceiling over one side of the seating creates intimacy, while elsewhere views upward reveal the diagonal timbers of the superstructure fading into the roof's volume. The master bedroom, overlooking the nook, hovers within the various volumes below and above, yet no sight line from any habitable

7.9 Moore house. The kitchen looking toward the little dining pavilion.

7.10 Moore house. The stair and second-floor bridge.

space intrudes on its privacy, while the enormous adjacent expanse of glass unites it with the trees and the bluff, the surf, and the Olympic Mountains, miles away on the horizon.

Thus by the early 1980s Bystrom had completed the "Black Angus" restaurant series and the Forward Thrust bathhouse adaptations, and had served the Pike Place Market in several roles. His earliest residential work had received several awards, and the unique character of his little Pacific coast cabin had brought him national recognition. He had embarked on a series of residential projects of remarkable quality and unusual inspiration, of which the Moore house is a vanguard example. These achievements were recognized in 1985 by his election to Fellowship in the American Institute of Architects.

7.11 Moore house. The master bedroom; a sleeping platform in a stave church, with the whole world in view.

The Dennis house in Sun Valley of the 1980s, introduced in the Prologue, and the subject of chapter 9, is the largest and most elaborate example of the stave-church family, although in the relationship of its cladding to its structure it is also atypical. It was followed by several smaller variations on the stave-church theme. One, untitled and undated, remained a project only. The plan is obviously derived from the Raft River retreat, with its diagonal axes of symmetry, while the structural and spatial envelope, deriving from the stave-church image, will serve as a prototypical study for several projects to follow. Of those, the cabin for James and Carolee Kempton, begun in 1991, is certainly one of the most interesting.

The Kempton cabin is sited on a narrow peninsula on Obstruction Island, a small island in the San Juan group. The peninsula is only about 120 feet wide, so water is in close proximity to the north, west, and south. The Olympic Mountain range makes up much of the horizon. The site obviously presents tremendous opportunities in richness of outlook; it also offers a degree of natural haven in the scattered stand of trees along the spine of the peninsula.

As so often in Bystrom's work, the plan of the Kempton cabin derives from a square, and, as usual, the square is physically manifested in the structural bay of four wooden columns. In this case the square is translated in two axes to create three cognate pavilions, connected by smaller square bridges. The pavilions can touch the ground lightly;[5] a pier at each corner suffices. The scheme minimizes disruption of

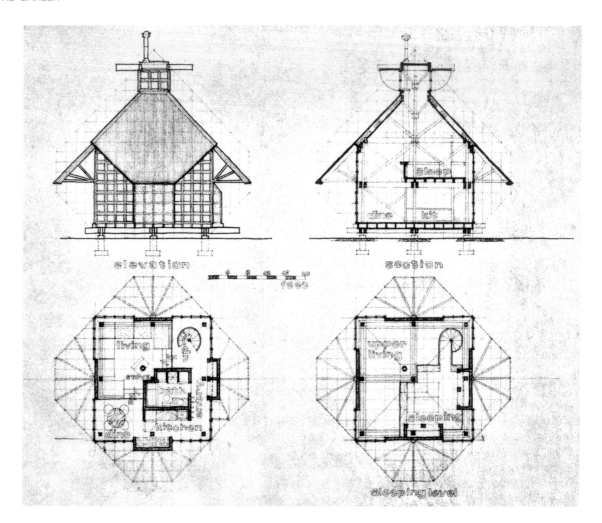

elevation

section

feet

living

dine   kitchen

sleep

dine   kit

upper
living

sleeping

sleeping level

*7.12 Bystrom, an
undated, untitled
project.*

existing trees, subdivides the already diminutive mass of the building, and satisfies the Kemptons' request that the living room double as a guest bedroom with appropriate privacy. It also allows Bystrom to explore three different orientations and moods.

At the time of its design, the Bystrom children had spent a summer or two at camp, and Bystrom had enjoyed the camp's straightforward organization—"a little cookhouse for cooking dinner in the center, surrounded by tents or cabins where they would live."[6] Hence the Kempton central pavilion houses kitchen and dining; it is open on three sides to a northwestern view and a northwest facing deck. To the southwest is the living pavilion, with a dramatic westward view and a west-

facing deck. Northeast of the dining pavilion is the bedroom. It alone turns its back on dramatic views; its windows open to the short vistas and the soft light of the woods at the centerline of the peninsula. Its deck is nestled into the trees. The bedroom, therefore, offers the greatest sense of haven. But the other two pavilions also suggest intimacy and enclosure because of the repetitive deep and dark volumes overhead, as well as the deep soffits over the decks that are created by the high and steep pyramidal roofs common to all the pavilions. The little pavilions are cheerfully anthropomorphic—three crowned and visored heads, studying the views.

The shared pyramidal roofs, of course, are the essence of the spatial and structural

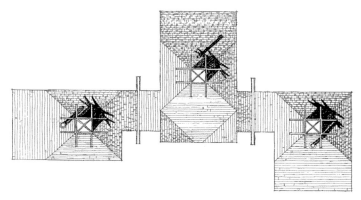

ROOF PLAN

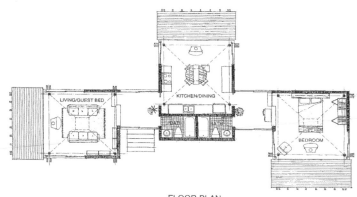

LIVING/GUEST BED

KITCHEN/DINING

BATH BATH

BEDROOM

FLOOR PLAN

concept. That concept begins with the idea of four posts—far too delicate, in this case, to encourage a convincing stave-church analogy— that establish the corners of a fifteen-foot square. The superstructure these posts will support derives from a conceptual geometry whose vertical dimensions are established by an eave line eight feet outboard of the posts and seven feet above the floor plane. From this datum a pyramidal volume, its sides at a 45 degree slope, may be realized in various permutations; the concept leaves Bystrom free to include or omit the eave projection on any face of any pavilion. Thus in the central pavilion Bystrom provides an eave to the northwest over the porch, and, on the opposite side, another to enclose the kitchen counter and cabinets and two baths, while from the other two faces partial eaves descend to become parts of the roofs over the adjacent bridges. The eave of the southwestern pavilion looks to the western sunset; the northeastern pavilion's eave peers southeastward into the trees. Furthermore, each of the pavilions rises from a different floor elevation, so the three pyramidal roofs begin at, and ascend to, three different heights, to which the three little lighting

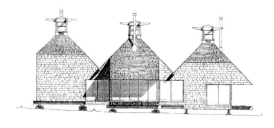

NORTH ELEVATION

7.13 Bystrom, James and Carolee Kempton cabin, Obstruction Island, 1991. Site plan.

7.14 Kempton cabin. Floor and roof plans.

7.15 Kempton cabin. Northwest and southeast elevations.

79

7.16 Kempton cabin. The approach from the east.

7.17 Kempton cabin. The exterior from the northwest, with the dining pavilion in the foreground.

and ventilating top hats draw our attention. The geometric complexity is resolved in the bridges, by allowing the roof planes to intersect off center. (Apart from their formal and experiential value, the porch overhangs also contribute structural rigidity: their sloping and horizontal ties to the posts lock the lower part of the structure against lateral deflection—an important issue on this windswept peninsula in an earthquake zone. And since the three pavilions connect to one another across the bridges, the rigidity of each is shared by all.) As was the case with the Moore house—and the stave church—enclosing surfaces lie outboard of the autonomous structural frame, and serve only as weather membranes.

Duo Dickenson has written of the Kempton cabin: "If this project were set on a barren hillside (as is a classic villa or farmhouse), these organizing features would be obvious—perhaps even problematically so. But set amid the wild growth of this windswept

7.18 Kempton cabin. The entry.

7.19 Kempton cabin. The central (dining) pavilion, looking northwest.

7.20 Kempton cabin. The bedroom, looking north.

7.21 *Kempton cabin. "There they are!"*

island, these two organizing principles [symmetry and modular construction] are simply not apparent."[7] Dickenson's analyses are perceptive, but reasonable people may differ. The organizing principles of the little pavilions seem entirely apparent on the existing site. They are compelling not because they are masked, but because of the skill with which Bystrom has made a seemingly rigid geometric and structural concept yield a remarkable flexibility and variety, without once compromising its discipline. Much of the delight, charm, even whimsy, of the little Kempton pavilions lies in their blatantly evident kinship and their equally evident saucy individuality. One visitor, approaching the project by boat, announced his sighting in the plural: "There they are!"[8]

A project of the following year, the smallest of the stave-church family, brings Bystroms's late career full circle. In 1992 Joel Connelly and Mickey Pailthorp asked Bystrom to design a cabin for their Whidbey Island site, a densely forested bluff with an eastward view to Puget Sound. Bystrom and the clients imagined "a tree house, a forest within a forest, a shrine of branches and light."[9] Connelly and Pailthorp had seen Bystrom's own cabin on the Washington coast, and clearly both they and the architect had in mind that little building of twenty years earlier. And at about twenty by twenty-four feet, the Connelly footprint is similarly minuscule. But the Connelly design was to be more than a clone.

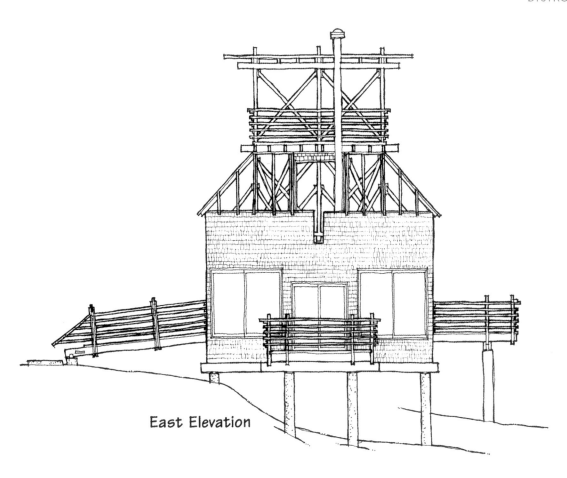

East Elevation

7.22 Bystrom, the
Joel Connelly and
Mickey Pailthorp
cabin, Whidbey
Island, 1992. East
elevation.

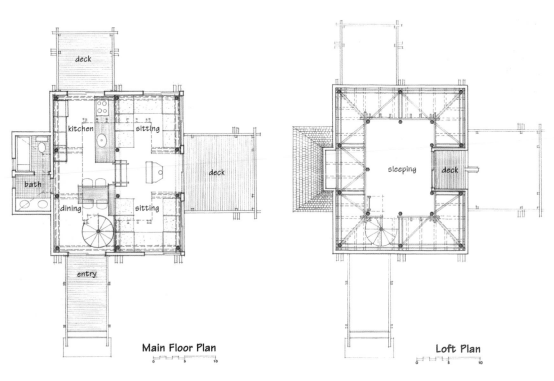

Main Floor Plan

Loft Plan

7.23 Connelly-
Pailthorp cabin. Main
floor and loft plans.

The topography of the site was to remain unmodified, and no significant flora were to be removed; thus the cabin is perched on a few cylindrical concrete posts. A bridge leads to the entry at the southwest corner, within which a circular stair provides access to the sleeping loft above; dining and kitchen lie ahead. The living space with fireplace occupies the entire eastern half of the cabin, its floor lower by two steps. From it a generous deck, with a beautifully detailed railing of bypass members, reaches out toward the Sound. The deck is about ten feet above the forest floor, and so is immersed in the branches of the surrounding conifers. Similar decks open to the north from the kitchen and to the east from the living space. The walls are simple shingled surfaces, within which sliding glass door units of repetitive sizes offer generous views. The only artificial heat source is a high-efficiency wood stove.

So far the description sounds much like

7.24 Connelly-Pailthorp cabin. The kitchen, overlooking the living space below, with the sleeping loft at upper right.

7.25 Gol Stavkirke. The chassis. (Drawing by T. William Booth.)

7.26 Connelly-Pailthorp cabin. An early study model of the structure.

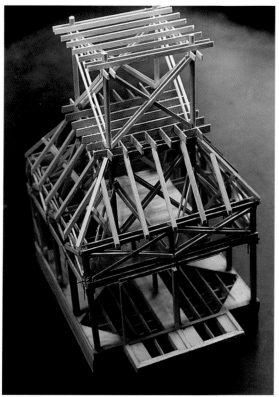

that of the Bystrom cabin. But there are differences. That the organizational axes are orthogonal rather than diagonal is only a minor point, as is the fact that the detached Bystrom privy has become a civilized Connelly bathroom, attached as a kind of architectural saddlebag. Much more important is the stave-church theme, which recurs here once again: lying inboard of the shingled exterior walls, twelve poles, octagonal this time, lead the eye upward to a complex bypass system of beams and joists, on which the floor of the sleeping loft floats. Above, an even more complex structure disappears beyond the loft. In this feature the real evolution of the theme is revealed. The lofts of the Bystrom cabin were under a glass roof; the Connelly loft is surrounded by one, whose complex composition of wood supporting members suggests the branches of the trees immediately beyond.

And since the edges of the loft floor are four feet inboard of the lower exterior walls, all the spaces of the lower floor also partake of this glass-and-branches roof—the "forest within a forest," the "shrine of branches and light." A trap door leads to the rooftop eyrie, for which the deck opening off the first floor was a precursor. This eyrie, a new and original whimsy in Bystrom's work, most fully realizes the tree house image. High above the forest floor, its architectural tree trunks and branches interweave with the living branches and foliage, through which the Sound can be seen in filtered glimpses far below.

7.27 Connelly-Pailthorp cabin. A structural detail at the upper exterior wall, from which the glass roof ascends.

7.28 Connelly-Pailthorp cabin. The living space.

7.29 Connelly-Pailthorp cabin. The sleeping loft.

7.30 Connelly-Pailthorp
cabin. From the southwest.

In 1997 Bystrom, like Thiry, Kirk, and Lovett before him, was awarded the AIA Seattle Medal for distinguished lifetime achievement.

8.1 *Lovett, the Charles*
Simonyi house, Villa
Simonyi, Medina,
1987–. The original
Villa, from the west.
(© Michael Jensen)

Wendell Lovett:
The Villa Simonyi

In 1987 Lovett began the design of a house on a Lake Washington waterfront site in Medina, a suburb of Seattle, for Charles Simonyi, who was then chief architect of research and development for Microsoft. Simonyi is also a collector of art, whose acquisitions were heavily weighted toward the paintings of his fellow Hungarian Victor Vasarely and the American Roy Lichtenstein. His aesthetic program was remarkable for its detail, and for its articulately expressed design challenges. His first priority, as he explained it, was "aesthetic quality . . . both as a set of exciting concepts and in form and execution. The observer will appreciate the visual art of Vasarely, the 'plastic' unity of form, color and textures; the tension resulting from the intrusion of dissonance into established order; and elements of surprise, discovery, mystery, and challenge."

The design of the house must include three "modes," private, family, and public, all spatially distinct from one another, with infrequent transition between the modes. "Transition would include a change in mood, activity, smell, sound, privacy, people seen, etc. The design should acknowledge the changes, just as a Moonbase must acknowledge a transition from the interior to the exterior." An elevator must "connect all levels, control access, and provide visual drama." The evident main entry must be austere: "There need not be any window in the entrance door or on the wall facing the street. I would typically enter through the garage. Business visitors would enter the [west] yard through steps in one of

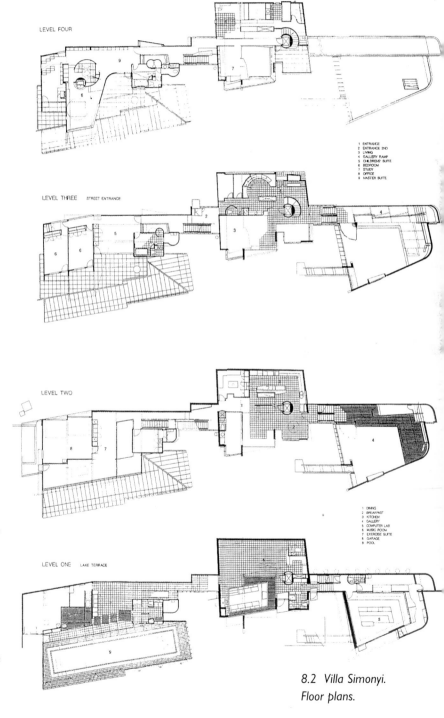

8.2 Villa Simonyi.
Floor plans.

the side setback areas. The remainder, intimate party visitors, would be the only people needing the entrance doors. Once inside, there could be some dramatic views to the west, to the south, and even to an interior private space, but without obvious access to these spaces."

The pragmatic program was similarly specific. Required were: a master bedroom ("a little cave") with bath; a private living space/library to accommodate thirty yards of books and a six-foot-square Vasarely; kitchen and dining; family/guest bedrooms and baths; a family space "with some view, maybe a continuation of the living/dining area"; a workshop with machine and woodworking tools; a pool, "not very large" but "rectangular"; and a hot tub "if it fits the architecture." Simonyi also requested an extensive party room—"we should be able to cram a live band in there"—with bath and shower, a bar, and a light cooking area.

The original Simonyi site was a single waterfront parcel. The shoreward part ascends in a reasonable slope for about half the site depth, then rises steeply through about twenty-five feet of height. Zoning required that a new structure be set well back from the

8.3 Villa Simonyi. Site plan.

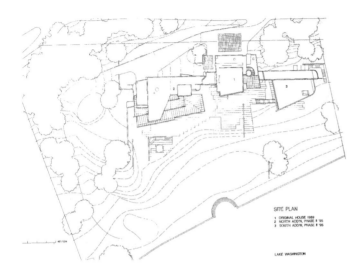

8.4 Villa Simonyi. The original dining room, looking north. Above, beyond the glass wall, is the small original gallery. The photograph was taken after the additions of 1993, when the space at center became dining; the table is by Carlo Scarpa. (© Michael Jensen)

8.5 Villa Simonyi. The original dining room, with the dining table of Lovett's design; see also fig. 1.6.

shoreline, hence against and into the bank. Thus a scheme of several stories was likely, with entry probably at a third level. Civic zoning restrictions determined front and side yard setbacks and a maximum height, and the building's footprint must be no more than 15 percent of the total site area. These limitations meant that the spatial demands of the program would claim almost all of the available volume. The building would, of necessity, approximate a cube.

The Original Villa

The first phase of what would become a far larger building was designed for that rather small site, and built on it in 1987-88. At some early date, on a simple subjective whim, Lovett began referring to the project as the Villa Simonyi, and the name has stuck.[1]

The first floor level of the original Villa was established at an elevation slightly above the west lawn. Much of the northern half of the west wall is skewed at an angle determined by the required shoreline setback. Immediately inside at the first level was the "rectangular" pool, actually a parallelogram in plan that echoes the skew of the western wall. Beyond, to the east, was the party room.

At the second level was a dining room, with view and access to the lawn and the lake. The circular dining table (now the breakfast table) is of Lovett's design, and is one of his finest pieces. Six cantilevering black steel arms end in rubber disks that support the glass top, and the disk faces can be adjusted to a common planarity by means of horizontal machine screws that bear against the face of the cylindrical base. The kitchen occupied much of the space to the east.

Above, at the third level, is a gallery, small in plan dimensions but of double height in its southern half, for display of several Vasarely pieces. Above the north half of the space, at the fourth or top level, is Simonyi's study; its

8.6 Villa Simonyi. The original gallery, looking northwest. (© Michael Jensen)

8.7 Villa Simonyi. The original gallery, looking southeast; the glass wall that overlooks the dining space is at far right; at center is the elevator cylinder with its red door. (© Michael Jensen)

8.8 Villa Simonyi. The original gallery, looking north. The glass wall over the dining space occupies the left half of this view. (© Michael Jensen)

teak-edged desk floats above the planes of the faceted balcony. Immediately east was Dr. Simonyi's bedroom and bath. At mid-height of the double-height space horizontal white half-cylinders cross the west and south walls; these house heating and cooling ducts, and are meant to express them. To the southwest a floor-to-ceiling glass wall in two planes overlooks the breakfast space below; its remarkable flush edge detailing deserves notice. To the east at

8.9 Villa Simonyi. The original gallery, looking south into the upper part of the dining space.

8.10 Villa Simonyi. The east facade, the "back." (© Michael Jensen)

the third level is the main entry from the drive.

Simonyi had emphasized that the elevator should be more than an occasional or expedient device, and Lovett has made it so. It is pragmatically necessary: stairs serve the third and fourth levels and a roof terrace, but descent to levels one and two, or ascent from either to level three, can be done only by elevator. The elevator is appropriately formally assertive: it is housed within a gray cylinder that penetrates through all floors, and it is entered at all floors through a bright red door.

Some of the design decisions in this original Villa were shaped by Simonyi's admiration for Vasarely's work, which Lovett shares. Vasarely's paintings, especially from the 1970s and 1980s, are typically compositions of meticulously drafted geometric shapes—parallelograms, squares, circles, and combinations thereof—arranged in a pattern, a part of which is often distorted. They create an illusion of a third dimension, and dazzle the retina as well. The Villa's design includes several direct references to the square, the circle, and the parallelogram (examples are the square panels of glazing, the round elevator housing and several door windows, and the parallelogram of the pool). The idea of distortion finds expression serendipitously in the deflected north half of the lake facade, and intentionally in the faceted balcony within the living space, and the other canted features that are most evident in the western elevation. Lovett's use of walls of glass, and reflective surfaces for floors, cabinets, and doors, was an attempt to encourage surprising multiple visual juxtapositions. Some other characteristics of the design are direct responses to Simonyi's wishes. The extremely understated entry facade, the most austere of Lovett's "backs," conforms to Simonyi's request. His program had emphasized, however, that the Villa's appearance from the lake was to be highly expressive, and the original Villa as seen from the west was, simply put, a beautiful composition.

Shortly after the completion of this design,

Simonyi acquired another lot roughly equivalent in size to the south and a quite extensive tract of land to the north. Major additions were built on these lands from 1993 to 1996, in a second phase of the Villa's history. At the same time, although the original Villa's exterior remained largely intact, several interior changes were made. The entry remained as it had been, but the space immediately north became a shoe-changing room and closet, for larger parties of visitors. The party room became a music room, for which the pool was converted to a listening area. The dining space became the breakfast space; the area to its north became a formal dining room, with a dining table of Carlo Scarpa's design. The kitchen was enlarged, and now occupies two-thirds of the eastern part of the second level.

The detailing of the revised kitchen, based on that of the original kitchen, establishes several characteristics of the ensuing project. Countertops and backsplash are granite in a soft blue coloration. Cabinet fronts are painted to auto body standards. The glass outline of the cabinets above the west sink conjoins Vasarely's circles with Vasarely's squares.

8.11 Villa Simonyi. From the western lawn. (© Michael Jensen)

8.12 Villa Simonyi. The kitchen as remodeled. The farther cabinets and wall are unchanged from the original phase; the entire counter composition at right, and that opposite it at left, are from the remodeling. (© Michael Shopenn)

8.13 Villa Simonyi. The kitchen as re-modeled. The glass in the gray cabinets at far right plays Vasarely games; the cantilevering channels are at left. (© Michael Shopenn)

8.14 Villa Simonyi. The exterior from Lake Washington. The original Villa is at center; the gallery is beyond the boat. The glass-enclosed pool is at left, at grade; the cantilevered master bedroom is above, far left. (© Michael Shopenn)

Under these cabinets a pair of steel channels, whose supporting devices are boldly declared, are outrageously cantilevered to the south to support a granite serving counter. The machine screws used for all exposed connections along these channels, and elsewhere in the kitchen, are torqued by a means familiar to users of fine cameras: two small cylindrical blind holes are let into an otherwise planar bolt face; a wrench with matching pegs applies the tightening force. This detail, hereafter called "snake-eyes," is used for the heads of exposed machine screws throughout the additions to north and south.

Now, we turn to those additions. As we do so, several points must be noted.

First, those additions are gathered around a circulation system that is organized with the utmost clarity, but is also of a complexity

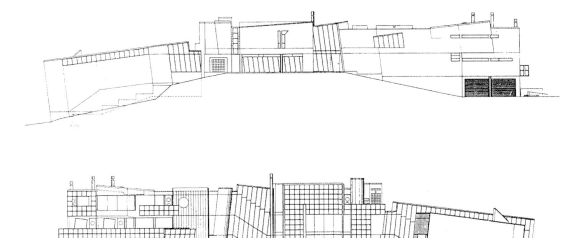

8.15 Villa Simonyi. East and west elevations including the additions of 1993-96.

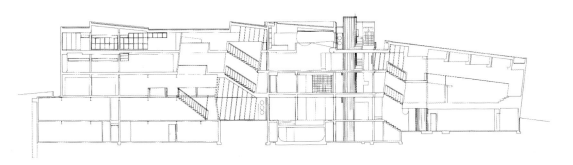

8.16 Villa Simonyi. North-south section.

unprecedented in Lovett's work. The original entry was in the east facade, where it remains, and another exterior door opens to the lawn and the lake on the west. These establish a four-level east-to-west circulation axis, whose midpoint, and vertical connector, is the elevator. The new additions are organized around north-south "go" spaces of considerable length that intersect the east-west axes at the elevator. Thus the Villa with its additions has four stacked levels of east-west and north-south axial paths of movement, all intersecting at the elevator shaft that symbolically and pragmatically comprises a vertical path. To this is added the supplemental vertical circulation of the stairs, just north and south of the original pavilion, that

belong to the north-south "go" space (see 8.2). This is a complex but clearly organized three-dimensional version of what was heretofore, in Lovett's practice, a single circulation path with typically only one or two floors of vertical interaction. The "street" metaphor is still appropriate, but the Simonyi street is no longer an architectural transformation of the simple, centuries-old vehicular and pedestrian path. A more appropriate metaphor would be the streets, overpasses, subways, elevators, escalators, and stairs that make up the complex circulation network of the modern city.

The additions were also informed by two visual metaphors. In the Puget Sound region southwest winds are prevalent, and they

95

8.17 *Villa Simonyi. From the west lawn, looking northeast; the gallery is at extreme right, the original villa is just right of center. (© Michael Shopenn)*

sweep across Lake Washington to beset the Simonyi site unchecked. Lovett imagined the extended Villa as leaning into these prevailing winds, visibly countering their force. Hence the additions are given a consistent southwestern inflection through permutations of two geometric features of the original Villa—the southern cant of its opaque south wing wall at the third level, and the plan deflection of its northern fenestration. Lovett also claims that in working out this theme he was guided by memories of Fernand Léger's painting *La Partie de la Campagne*; he thought of the Villa as

Léger's reclining human figure.

The Southern Wing: The Gallery and Computer Laboratory

A short flight of the south stair leads to a balcony that overlooks the gallery. Both stair and balcony are remarkable for their luxuriantly mechanistic detailing. The stair handrail is held by a clip that engages the balustrade. The balustrade—a grid of flat stainless steel bars—is an upward extension of a stainless steel micro-truss, consisting of flat bar stock and a compression tube, that supports the teak treads. The assembly of truss/grid and handrail is connected, in turn, to posts attached to window mullions on one side, and to mounting plates that are machine screwed to the wall surface on the other. The geometry of each piece is milled to complement and interlock with its neighbor.

The balustrade's overall geometry derives from the original Villa's skewed wall planes and its third-floor wing wall, and the intrinsic requirement of stairs that their treads must overlap one another by an inch or two. These considerations, taken together, suggested the inclined "verticals" of the balustrade. It then seemed appropriate that the adjacent window mullions echo this inclination, since at night, and during certain daytime conditions, the stair is seen through the glass wall. The mullions, in turn, determined the inclination of the "shower tower," which thereby accords with the geometric skews of the original Villa, as the entire composition is seen from the west.

The quarter-circle balcony just beyond is cantilevered by means of five steel arms, pivoted at the column connection and suspended by stainless steel rods attached to the arms by means of adjustable stainless steel clevises. Since the clevises engage the arms near the column, inboard of the balcony's floor surface, the top edge of each arm is in tension, the bottom in compression; accordingly, a flange is provided along the bottom edge to resist buckling. The shapes of these elements, and the shapes of the vertical members holding the balcony rail, recall the helical-stair details of the long-ago Hilltop remodeling. All machine screw connections are exposed, and detailed with snake-eye torquing holes.

Beyond the balcony, a ramp descends at a 7 degree slope, determined for reasons of comfort, which entirely by chance is perpendicular to the cant of the wing wall at the third level of the original Villa. The ramp's slope determines that of the roof, the north wall,

8.18 Villa Simonyi. The stair from the original gallery to the new one.

8.19 Villa Simonyi. A detail of the stair handrail.

8.20 Villa Simonyi. The balcony: the connection to the column, and the tension rods with clevis attachment, from above.

8.21 Villa Simonyi. The balcony from below, looking northeast.

and several other formal elements of the gallery addition. The ramp, the last southward element of the north-south circulation axis, is itself a remarkable sculpture of form, space and light. Its ceiling is comprised of boxes of light, and at the end of the vista the wall is washed with western light (fig. 8.2, level-three plan, far right). The offset in the rail at the third-point of its length, necessitated by the storeroom below, is a sculptural gesture of great success. As the ramp approaches the southern wall, two short flights of stairs

quicken the last phase of the descent, turning the path back to the north, toward the body of the gallery. Thus the long "go" space, returning on itself, becomes a "stop" space of grand dimension.

The tilted northern wall alone is glazed, providing ideal light for a gallery; it is balanced by light from the ramp light boxes, a north-facing monitor over the stage, and a limited western window whose jambs, sill, and head are withdrawn into the space. The east and south wall, and the south and west wall, curved at the corners, are continuous surfaces, almost entirely opaque, that wrap and enfold the space. Their purpose is to shield the artwork from direct sun. In doing so they mask a potential view of tremendous depth to the west and south, and that view is further masked by the door in the north wall and the ramp leading to the lawn. The dominant view from the gallery is the much shorter vista along the west facade of the Villa itself. Thus the gallery is also a cave, though a paradoxically large one, as is appropriate to its semipublic but internally focused purposes, and to its role as the closure of the long north-south axis.

The skew of the west wall, like that of the original Villa, is determined by the required setback from the water line. The combination of the skew and the curved corners, however, yields a plan shape much like that of the sitting room in the Scofield house, and similar, too, to that of a house by Ralph Erskine that Lovett had seen published in *Domus,* before his long-ago Stuttgart year.

The gallery is primarily a showplace for Simonyi's collection of paintings, and second-arily a theater for spoken and occasional musical performances; the room's nonparallel surfaces and ceiling baffles are intended to enhance acoustic quality.

Below the gallery is a computer labora-tory. This is a particularly twenty-first-century working arena, whose elegance is at the

8.22 Villa Simonyi.
The balcony and the
new gallery ramp,
looking northeast.
(© Michael Shopenn)

8.23 Villa Simonyi.
The new gallery,
looking southeast.
(© Michael Shopenn)

8.24 Villa Simonyi. The view from the new gallery to the northern addition.

on the exterior, and detailed like that to the gallery, leads to the various levels of the northern addition. The pool and its supporting spaces occupy the lowest level.

The pool, of sixty-foot length (eighteen meters), is housed within a glass shell supported by a richly complex steel armature. Lovett's interest in the expression of structure dates from at least his college years, and the roof beams of the Reed house of 1955 are an early example from his professional career. He found encouragement in the thought of Fritz Leonhardt at Stuttgart, and subsequently studied the work of Robert Maillart. For the Simonyi pool Lovett acknowledges an inspiration from the more recent work of Santiago Calatrava. Lovett's admiration for Calatrava is grounded in more than formal appeal. Calatrava, trained as both architect and engineer, derives his architectural forms largely from contemplation of structure, but the structures he contemplates are as much Darwinian as Newtonian. Calatrava combines a thoroughly sophisticated grasp of mathematically based engineering with an equally sophisticated study of the engineering of animals— how the structures of lions, wolves, whales, beetles, and birds have evolved to a perfected efficiency. From these reflections he has made a remarkable architecture of bones and muscle, inventiveness and grace. To such a process, and such a result, Lovett, of course, is deeply sympathetic, given his own long-standing interest in the biological and psychological sources of form. Lovett's homage to Calatrava in the architecture of the Simonyi pool, therefore, is a homage to method, and only incidentally to form.

The floor of the exercise room above, and the children's terrace above that, overhang the pool area by about six feet. Paired columns along the edge of the pool area support beams that cantilever to carry the overhanging floors. Each column pair is aligned on the normal

service of serious functional purposes. The many computer stations that command the center of the room inevitably suggest Simonyi's "Moonbase." Most of the surrounding wall surfaces are sliding chalkboard panels, including the west wall, whose panels can close the western view, to focus and support intense working sessions.

The Northern Wing: The Pool and Exercise Rooms

North of the original pavilion a stair, expressed

north-south grid of the house; alignment between pairs of columns parallels the skew of the pool itself. The planes established by these paired columns are glazed. The glass, mortised into the floor and ceiling planes with no visible trim, does a little side-step at each column pair to accommodate the geometric translation. The dichotomous geometry is also found in the alignment of shapes, and between shapes, of the four teak floor inserts east of the paired columns (see figs. 8.2, 8.26). At the western edge of the pool, steel beams are poised on a range of tripods. Such a beam, simply supported at each end, is under the greatest bending stress at and near the center of its span. The upper and lower flanges of the beam do the real work in withstanding such a stress, and the farther the flanges are separated from one another, the easier is their task. Accordingly the upper and lower flanges of these

8.25 Villa Simonyi. The new gallery as seen from the southwest lawn.

8.26 Villa Simonyi. The stair linkage to the northern addition. This run leads down to the pool level; the balcony at upper right leads to the second level exercise suite.

beams are most widely separated in the middle two-thirds of the span, and the vertical web, whose only task in this area is to keep the flanges apart, is perforated—a permutation of the roof beams of the Reed house (see fig. 2.17). As the structure turns the southwest corner, these concepts are elaborated in diagonal relationships. This is not the most straightforward way to support a glass roof over a pool. But it is beautifully expressive of the way each part goes about its daily tasks, and it manages to achieve as well a vertebrate skeletonic quality appropriate to Lovett's inspiration.

8.27 Villa Simonyi. The swimming pool and its foyer. (© Michael Shopenn)

8.28 Villa Simonyi. The pool, looking west toward the lake.

8.29 Villa Simonyi. The pool, looking north. (© Michael Shopenn)

The "Shower Tower" and the Children's Suite

The most interesting of the shower tower bathrooms is the children's bath at the third level, a charmingly ambivalent room of bright colors and crisp geometric shapes, adjacent to the children's play space and bedrooms.

The Master Bedroom and Library

The exterior of the master bedroom suite is unique among the Villa's elements in having an overhanging roof which, taken together with the treatment of wall surfaces and fenestration, immediately suggests a 1950s modernist suburban house. Within, any such interpretation is foreclosed by the skewed relationships of the walls, and the revisiting of the cylinder, in the plan of the closet and its interlocking fireplace, and, inferentially, in the geometry of the bed. The bed itself is rectangular, but it is part of a rotating platform that can turn toward the fireplace, the TV, or the view to

8.30 Villa Simonyi.
The children's bath.

8.31 Villa Simonyi.
The master bedroom
foyer. (© Michael
Shopenn)

the lake. Accordingly, the attached headboard is, in plan, an arc of the circumscribed circle; it meshes with its concave negative in the fixed headboard. The craftsmanship of the fixed and movable elements is remarkable.

Immediately north of the bedroom is the library, a space of intimate plan dimensions, with a low ceiling, three opaque walls, and a prominent fireplace. The library, closing the reach of the northern "go" space, is the ultimate place of repose, a private cave that complements the quasi-public cave, the gallery, far to the south. Beyond the library's fireplace the one glazed wall opens to an elevated terrace and a magnificent view of the lake. The description inevitably recalls Lovett's little Crane Island retreat a quarter of a century earlier. But there is a difference, and it is an important one. The deck of the Crane Island retreat offers a nearly hemispherical cone of vision; the truss chord slopes to nothing, for the deck has no rail. The Villa's library terrace, on the other hand, is shaded by a deep over-hang above, and, toward the view, is screened by a wall of Vasarely squares through which a concise opening has been cut. There is a germane analogy. The palazzi that front Venice's broad and busy Grand Canal invari-ably include a balcony, at a similar height, withdrawn into the body of the palazzo, with a balustrade, robust columns, and richly fretted

spandrels in the plane of the facade. Those characteristics are more than ornamental: since the balcony is well above the surface of the canal, the floor plane and the balustrade intercept sight lines from passing gondolas, while the deep shade of the recess, and the visual intervention of the columns, further screen the balcony's occupants from uninvited observation. Lake Washington too is a heavily used body of water, and the Villa Simonyi is a conspicuous object at its edge. The design of the library terrace provides its dwellers both outlook and privacy.

The Villa Simonyi:
Some Closing Observations

When they first discussed adding to the original Villa, Simonyi and Lovett agreed that the additions need not emulate the existing building, that the project, when completed, should communicate "something of its history . . . and should not attempt to conceal in a false unity its natural evolution."[2] The most obvious differences between the earlier and the later work are easily seen in the plans of the various

8.32 Villa Simonyi.
The master bedroom
looking east.
(© Michael Shopenn)

levels (fig. 8.2). The original Villa, for all its geometric richness, is the simpler part of the composition; it appears in the plans as an almost elemental Euclidean cube. The additions, by comparison, are much more geometrically complex. The differences are in part a result of program and site conditions. The program for the original Villa required the entire available volume of a constrained site. The southern gallery's site is equally constrained, but the program was more resilient, while the detailed program for the northern wing enjoys an expansive site.

The complexity of the additions is also a consequence of Lovett's acceptance of a greater formal and spatial freedom during the years that separate the phases. This is in part a result of continuing reflection on the multitude of his own thoughts and influences that will

have accrued over his many decades of practice. And it will be remembered too that he had mentioned, in connection with the Cutler-Girdler project, the sense of liberation he had drawn from the work of Gehry and Liebeskind, and he acknowledges a similar stimulus from other contemporaneous colleagues.

Lovett's late freedom, however, is distinctive in that it uncompromisingly serves his theoretical canons of anthropomorphic gesture, movement and repose, cave and meadow. These canons apply, above all, to the shaping of interior space. Thus Lovett's freedom is realized in concert with the modernist tenet that the appropriate composition of interior space is a paramount source of architectural form.

Lovett's late freedom is distinctive, too, in

that it is realized within a formal and spatial structure that pervades the entire architectural fabric—pervades even the various decades of Lovett's career. That this is true is attested by the fact that, for all their differences, the original Villa and its additions will seem, even to an initiated viewer, a remarkably coherent composition. The governing formal and spatial structure of the Villa Simonyi is determined by Lovett's theoretical canons noted above, and is augmented by the pervasive limited palette of high-tech materials and details, the four-level cross-axial "street" system that pinwheels from the elevator shaft, the reiterated Vasarely geometries, and the reiterated skewing of planes and volumes. This ordering structure integrates a highly complex design; it also bring us back to Lovett's lifelong interest in music.

Analogies between music and architecture are legion; the analogy that is perhaps most easily defended is that each is a manifestation of complex order.[3] All of Lovett's mature work— the Cutler-Girdler house is a remarkable example—might be so described in varying degree, as might all of Bystrom's, and indeed all architecture of long-standing reputation. The definition is especially appropriate to the Villa Simonyi with its additions in place. Thus the Villa does not "conceal in a false unity its natural evolution" but rather, like music, reveals a unity of thematic structure—complex indeed, and ordered too.

8.33 Villa Simonyi.
(Rendering by
Slava Simontov)

8.34 Villa Simonyi. The view from the northwest lawn; the master bedroom and its terrace are at upper left. (© Michael Shopenn)

Client, Design Associates, Consultants, Contractors, and Special Suppliers

Client	Dr. Charles Simonyi
Architect	The Wendell Lovett Architects
	Wendell Lovett FAIA, Charles J. Williams III, Associate with Susana Covarrubias, Keith Howell, Gordon Walker, and John Majewski
Structural Engineer	Robert Albrecht PE
Civil Engineer	Reid Middleton & Associates
Geotechnical Engineer	Neil Twelker & Associates

Landscape Architect	Henri Stoll
Contractor	Krekow Jennings Inc.
Cabinetwork	Stusser Woodworks
Furnishings	Gallery chairs: "Ekstrem," Terje Ekstrom for Stokke, Norway
	Music room seating: "Babilonia," by Dema, Italy
	Dining table: "Doge," Carlo Scarpa for Simongavina, Italy
	Breakfast table: Wendell Lovett
	Dining and breakfast chairs: "Sedia," Noto, Italy
	Library and office sofas: "Flu-flu," DePaz, D'Urbino, Lamozzi for Linge Roset, France
	Master suite: revolving bed, Wendell Lovett; bed lamps, "Zed," Lumina, Italy

9.1 Bystrom, the Reid and Peggy Dennis house, Sun Valley, Idaho, 1982-86. The exterior from the south. (© University of Washington Libraries, Special Collections)

Arne Bystrom:
The Dennis House

In 1979 Bystrom had submitted his Raft River vacation retreat for a national AIA award. It survived to a short listing, at which point, all projects under consideration had to be visited by a selected representative of the AIA jury. Ian Mackinlay came up from San Francisco to see the little building. He found a lot to admire and successfully argued its case for an Honor Award. A few years thereafter, in the fall of 1982, Mackinlay's longtime friend Reid Dennis, intending to build, asked Mackinlay to suggest an architect. Mackinlay suggested Bystrom.

Peggy and Reid Dennis wanted to build on their Sun Valley property a "normal-sized house" utilizing state-of-the-art solar energy technology. They had seen several such houses, however, and all seemed harsh in materials and detailing. They asked Bystrom to design an energy-conserving house that would also be "attractive, inviting—one would want to go inside, and when inside one would be happy to be there." As the design progressed the program grew significantly, eventually becoming a scheme of three zones: to the west, the Dennises own quarters, consisting of living and dining spaces, kitchen, and master bedroom suite; east of these, a guest zone of four bedrooms for visiting family and friends; and, at the far eastern end, a garage, studio, and storage.

The program, then, was extensive; the conceptual basis for its enclosure was relatively concise. A poured concrete foundation establishes floors and terraces at several levels that follow, to a considerable extent, the existing plateaus of the land. In many locations concrete walls extend upward from the floors and terraces. On this base, cylindrical columns are ranged in two parallel lines to support a great shed of roof. Its northern edge lies just above an earth berm, from which it rises in three folded planes to a southern eave. Its slopes were established by the angle of the sun's rays at the winter solstice but they seem to emulate the angle of repose of the surrounding geology: "The form of the roof echoes and evokes the surrounding hills."[1] Under the southern part of this roof a single space runs from the west end of the roof itself to the west end of the garage, and from concrete floor slab to underside of roof; at the west end this space, designated the living area, occupies the entire front-to-back dimension of the house. Under the northern part of the roof, the living area excepted, a seemingly inserted building within a building contains all the other programmed spaces, arranged in two stories. At the far eastern end this element terminates in a garage and, above, a caretaker's studio apartment.

To this relatively simple description,

9.2 Dennis house. The exterior from the east. (© University of Washington Libraries, Special Collections)

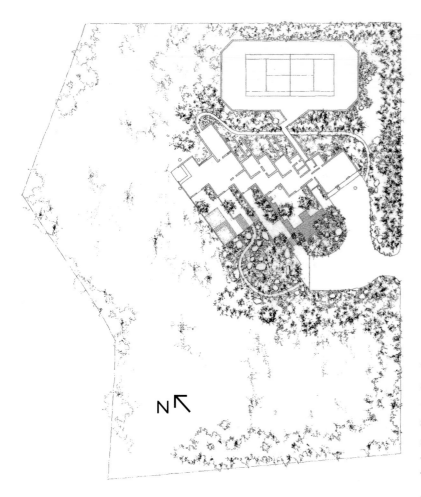

N↖

9.3 Dennis house. The site plan.

ops his plans from a square or, as in this case, a grid of squares. He acknowledges that this habit came from his admiration for Wright, who used such a grid as a design device for many of the Prairie Houses and Usonians, and all of the California block series. But a grid is a difficult design tool. Its discipline resists the variegated features inherent in any architectural problem; yet, if casually compromised, it loses its value as a cohering device. The larger the constituent unit, the more severe the problem; hence Wright's squares are small, varying from a bit over two feet to about four feet. Bystrom's are big; the Kempton cabin's is fifteen feet on a side. How does one secure malleability with a large modular unit? Bystrom does so in several ways. In the Kempton plan he created a boundary zone—the eave projection—that he could add, or not, on any face of any square.[2] The footprint of the Raft River cabin is a square, and the living space and entry are squares within, though of different dimensions, but elsewhere he has freely subdivided the cabin's geometry to suit structure or use. The Moore house grid seems to consist of cognate squares, but no "square" is really square: Bystrom has adjusted dimensions to suit plan requirements, and gains additional options by inventing the projecting pavilions. In the Connelly plan no "square" is, again, square, although the geometry is symmetrical about two axes.

The Dennis plan, however, includes two grids, and thus two different geometric concepts: that of the columnar structure, and that of the interior and exterior walls. They differ in purposes, dimensions, and orientation. Yet each has been made to accommodate the other, and to resolve the geometric challenges of an extraordinarily complex composition. How has this been accomplished? The walls, as we have seen, are governed in their exact alignment and location by the grid that aligns with the cardinal directions. In this case,

however, a considerable complication was introduced by the dimensions and orientation of the site. When the design was begun, the Dennises owned only a single lot whose configuration dictated that the long axis of the house be northwest-southeast. (They later bought an adjacent second lot to the southwest, and a part of one to the northeast.) Ideally, however, the actual facades of the enclosed spaces should face south for solar advantage, while choice views, and of course sunsets, are to the west. These considerations led Bystrom to orient the great roof roughly northwest-southeast, but to introduce, under it, a grid twisted by about 30 degrees to align with the cardinal directions; this "twisted" grid would determine all exterior and interior walls.

We have seen that Bystrom often devel-

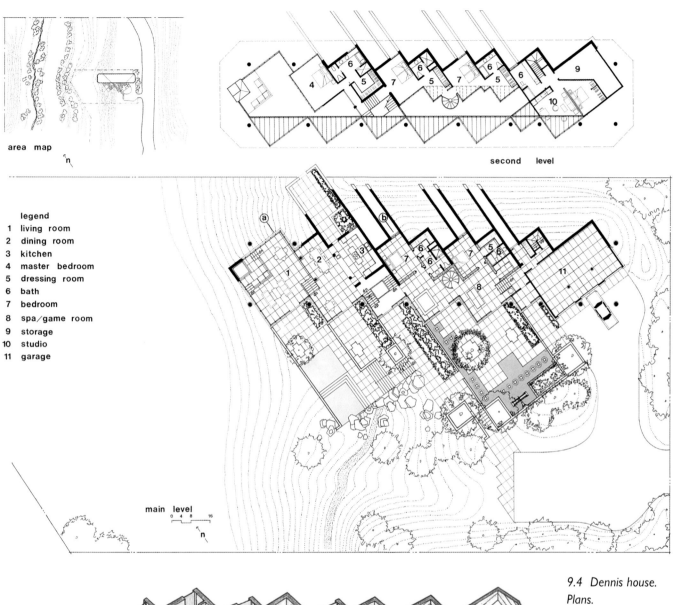

area map

second level

legend
1 living room
2 dining room
3 kitchen
4 master bedroom
5 dressing room
6 bath
7 bedroom
8 spa/game room
9 storage
10 studio
11 garage

main level
0 4 8   16

9.4 Dennis house.
Plans.

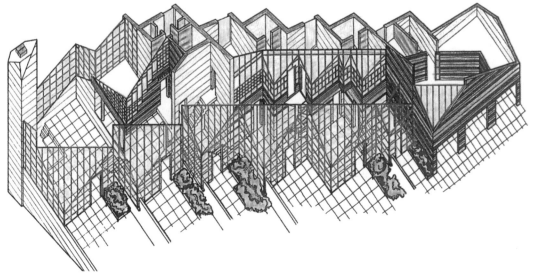

9.5 Dennis house.
Axonometric study.

9.6 Dennis house. The exterior from the south.

9.7 Dennis house. The exterior from the southwest.

9.8 Dennis house. The typical juncture of column and roof.

however, the grid is of small unit dimension—the squares are three feet on a side—and so is amenable to many dimensional possibilities; the walls can be of whatever configuration is appropriate to their purpose, with only minor adjustments to conform to the grid's demands. On the other hand, the northwest-southeast longitudinal centerlines of the great cylindrical wooden columns are absolute, because the columns must align with the two great pairs of beams that carry the roof. But along the southwestern of these centerlines, Bystrom has varied the column spacings to suit the undulations of the grid-controlled wall system, while on the northeastern centerline he omits all columns but three, supporting the intervening roof on the grid-determined concrete walls that occur there. Thus the column locations can shift to conform to the necessary configurations of the walls, and the walls, in turn, can accommodate the activities they envelop, and at the same time can dodge about the columns as necessary.

There is yet another geometric matter to be reckoned with, of course, for in architecture there is always a third dimension: the two geometries of the plan must meet the roof. The Dennis roof slopes; it slopes in three directions; and its three planes intersect in diagonal ridges. The problems arising from this geometry are resolved serendipitously.[3]

Although, as we have seen, the roof and the wall grid do not share the same orientation, in the following discussions, for simplicity, and unless exact orientation is crucial, we will describe all orientations as east and west, north and south.

The Structure

Heretofore Bystrom had typically used solid stock logs for cylindrical columns. The major columns of the Dennis house, however, are turned from laminated stock; they are eighteen inches in diameter. A few feet from the top of

each column, shoulder blocks support four struts that reach upward to the roof structure, and there is an elaborate bracket at the column top whose two stages cleverly accommodate either the horizontal or the sloping beams. The struts "suggest the natural canopy of a tree,"[4] and they and the brackets are also intended to "reference the great roofs of China and Japan, the houses of the Swiss Alps, the mast-framed stave churches of Norway, and of course the

9.9 Dennis house. From the dining level looking west toward the living space, with the fireplace at center. (© Michael Jensen)

9.10 Dennis house. From living space looking southeast toward the dining space, with the master bedroom eyrie above. (© University of Washington Libraries, Special Collections)

113

9.11 Dennis house. From the living space looking south toward Peggy Dennis's favorite spot, the little breakfast peninsula at left center that overlooks two terraces.
(© Michael Jensen)

residences of Greene and Greene."[5] The struts and brackets, however, do little or no structural work here, and where the struts would intercept glazed planes, they are cut away to allow glazing to continue uninterrupted. Steel plates in the undersides of the beams transfer loads directly from beams to column.[6]

Inside, in the dining room, four much smaller columns, footed on wood disks and with brackets but no struts, support the master bedroom above; two more in the garage support the caretaker's apartment. The floors of the upper guest bedrooms essentially rest on concrete walls, or concrete with some intervening woodwork. The roof consists of the primary paired beams already mentioned, and secondary beams with purlins above, surmounted by a cold-roof construction that minimizes heat gain and loss. The northern concrete walls resist lateral loads; the roof plane transfers rigidity throughout the structure.

The Living Room and the High Southern Space

To the south along almost the entire length of the house is the double-height sunlit space that at the west descends and continues northward to become the living space; its far west corner is a prow that reaches westward almost to the roof's edge, and is anchored by the fireplace. The fireplace is an integral part of a concrete substructure that encompasses terraces, interior floors, the vertical surfaces necessitated by the many changes of floor level, and many walls, especially to the north. All horizontal surfaces are ground and polished, and include ornamental strips of glazed tile and wood on a three foot module in both directions; at the east edge of the living space the tiles continue vertically up the wall, and coordinate with cabinetwork integral to that wall. Vertical concrete surfaces are sandblasted to expose the aggregate.

Elsewhere, vertical concrete surfaces,

including the fireplace, have horizontal bands of tile or wood at a two-foot module. All of these ornamental bands are finish work, set into recesses cast into the concrete at the time of pouring; they are in many cases modularly coordinated with other wall finish materials, door heads, and cabinetwork. This means that the earliest constructional work on the site—fabricating and locating the concrete forms, pouring the concrete, and screeding and troweling its surfaces—all of this work demanded execution to cabinetwork tolerances. That such extraordinary tolerances were achieved is a tribute to the architect's supervision, the contractor's patient diligence, and an astonishing level of craftsmanship put forward by the workmen.

The exterior wall of this space is of metal-framed glass, the lower half of which consists of six triangular peninsulas on the twisted grid. These peninsulas exist in part to accommodate staircases and the configurations of rooms to the north, and in part to create an upper living room, a breakfast pavilion, a hot tub area, a TV area, and the several entries to the house. The triangular glass roofs of the peninsulas rise to meet a single upper plane of glazing that parallels the roof beams, thus providing a tidy juncture.

The glass is argon-filled Alpenglass with Heat Mirror; the computer-controlled uppermost panes vent excess summer heat, while computer-controlled venetian blinds—the finely grained horizontal white strips—admit or reject the sun as appropriate. The translucent exterior sail-like panels that seem to float above the peninsulas are suspended Phillips evacuated-tube collectors that transmit accrued solar energy through pipes to heat storage tanks in the northern basement. These tanks redistribute heat to the floor slab as needed; fin-tube radiators below the glass augment the system. Warm air that gathers under the roof is drawn into the large white

vertical tube in the east end of the space, and returned to a rock bed under the slab, to again begin its warming journey. An evaporation pool, an evaporative cooler, and an air handler, all in the northern basement, provide forced ventilation and cooling.

Now, the stairs. All stairs in the house occur within this southern space. Several serve half-level changes of floor plane, and are straightforward. The system of half-flights and landings west of the hot tub, and the cylinder east of it, are not. They are the most extrava-

9.12 Dennis house. The western stair, an autonomous structural unit that accesses all levels of the house. (© Michael Jensen)

9.13 Dennis house. The southern space looking east, with the eastern lower bedroom at left, the helical stair ahead, and a corner of the hot tub at lower right.

9.14 Dennis house. The helical stair. (© Michael Jensen)

9.15 Dennis house. The southern space. (© Michael Jensen)

gantly dramatic elements in the house; each is a tour de force of wood craftsmanship.

The half-flights and landings, as they appear on plan, indicate the stair that connects the hot tub and dining levels of the main floor, continuing downward to access two lower levels, and upward an additional half-flight to meet a cantilevered half-flight that leads to an upper-floor guest bedroom. Apart from the uppermost cantilevered half-flight, this entire stair is an independent unit of construction that includes the landings. The vertical wood pieces that underlie the handrails form, in effect, a bearing wall; horizontals are laced across these, at a spacing dimension that allows them to bypass and so support the treads. Above, at the main levels, are handrails that are, in a sense, glulam beams, though glulams of unusual beauty, with core laminations of redwood and tops and bottoms of fir. At each end of each rail a short horizontal run anticipates a vertical

9.16 Dennis house. The dining space. (© University of Wash-ington Libraries, Special Collections)

9.17 Dennis house. The dining table and a chair.

downward return. At this 90 degree miter, as it were, the fir outer laminations are in fact mitered, but the interior redwood laminations are not; they terminate at the faces of small square fir pegs. This detail is repeated for handrails throughout the house.

The uppermost half-flight of this stair repeats the rail and tread detail below, but seems to be supported by fans of struts cantilevering from the concrete wall. These fans originally were intended to be structural, but Bystrom and the craftsmen worried that shrinkage in the struts would compromise the stair. Since the crucial shrinkage would be in the direction of the grain, therefore minuscule, it is likely that the struts continue to do a good bit of structural work. But to ensure absolute rigidity, the treads are also suspended from the rail, which at the lower end bears on the "wall" of wooden verticals, and at the top is anchored, by circuitous paths, to the concrete.

It is tempting to call the helical stair within

9.18 Dennis house. The kitchen as seen from the dining space. (© Michael Jensen)

9.19 Dennis house. The western lower floor bedroom.

9.20 Dennis house. The master bedroom, with the living space beyond and below.

9.21 Dennis house. The western of the two upper guest bedrooms. The ladder at center accesses a door, as beautifully detailed as the one in view, that leads to a storage loft over the master bath.

the cylindrical grille a straightforward permutation of the stair just described, but "straightforward" hardly seems the right word. The panel above the entry to this stair, and the circumferential top rail, repeat the typical rail design, but of course must arc on plan, as must all the circular elements. Each circular member is made up of several thin vertical laminations, steamed, bent, and glued, to assist in obtaining a true arc, and to obviate internal stresses within each piece that might, over time, lead to distortion. Each tread is made of alternating wedges of cherry and maple, a daunting joinery exercise in itself. Inboard ends of the treads are mortised into the central post, while outboard ends are bypassed, and therefore secured, by both the vertical and the horizontal pieces that make up the cylinder. Each juncture of this construction, taken independently, is exacting; all dimensional errors are cumulative vertically and radially; and the geometry of the entire system must close, on module, both vertically and circumferentially.

The Dining Room and the Kitchen

The north edge of the large southern volume is established by the two-story composition that includes a dining space, a kitchen, and five bedrooms. All of these spaces are intimate in scale; all are executed in astonishing wood craftsmanship.

The dining space occupies a plateau overlooking the living space; it is also open to the south, to the large southern volume and the terrace and landscape beyond. Yet the dining area itself is warmly intimate. Its ceiling, the underside of the master bedroom above, is a finely grained pattern of wood members that establish a vertical dimension sharply contrasting with that of the adjacent far higher space. The northern limit of the dining space is established by the concrete wall; the lateral edges are articulated by pairs of beams and the columns that support them.

Between the paired beams to either side are concealed lights that illuminate the edges of the space; lights within the ceiling members illuminate the table. The table and chairs, in walnut, with mother-of-pearl inlays inspired by Art Nouveau, were designed by Bystrom especially for the house. They were built by Evert Sodergren, a Seattle craftsman, also obviously of Scandinavian ancestry, who has made fine furniture for half a century.

The dining space is open to the kitchen across a countertop of a unique rust-hued vein of granite, two inches in thickness, with a honed working surface. The openness between kitchen and dining is typical of much recent home design, but the quality of kitchen materials and details gives this instance a unique elegance. All cabinet door faces include twenty-nine pieces, drawers twenty-five, closet doors thirty-five, in vertical grain fir and redwood; the small dark squares typical throughout are end-grain redwood inserts which, when oiled, darken to a walnut value. Each individual door and drawer pull includes nine pieces. This cabinetwork, executed by Boise Molding and Milling, is typical, in materials, design, and workmanship, of all cabinetwork throughout the house.

The Lower Bedrooms

The lower bedrooms have few windows to the north, and southern windows to the two-story volume beyond only above eye level. The absence of outlook, and the low level of natural light, are balanced by the richness of coloration and detail in the tile-banded concrete walls, the wood ceilings, and the window and door details. The rooms are, in fact, delightful cozy retreats, needing no apology for their introspective ambience.

The Master Bedroom and Bath

The second-floor spaces—the master bedroom and two guest bedrooms—nestle under the beams and purlins of the roof, and look out to the two-story volume through generous

9.22 Dennis house. The western upper bedroom, the "cave under the big roof," looking toward the meadow under the big roof, with vestibule closets at center. The helical stair is beyond at far right.

9.23 Dennis house. The guest bedroom vestibule closets and drawers.

9.24 Dennis house. The western upper bath; a typical detail.

expanses of glass in several planes. Though all three upper bedrooms are of about the same size, the master bedroom is, at the occupant's option, the most open. It overlooks the living space below through two planes of operable sash that continue without interruption to the underside of the roof; but sail-like white shades, concealed in the window sills, can be drawn upward for privacy or to screen the valley's sun. Several analogies for this space come to mind. Perhaps a luxurious tree house, or the bridge of a wooden ship, is most apt.

The Upper Guest Bedrooms
Are Oyasaeter, a student of Bystrom's work, has called the two upper guest bedrooms "cabins or caves under the big roof";[7] Bystrom has referred to them as "the final cave-like recesses."[8] They are similar but not identical. The south wall of sash in the western bedroom rises uninterrupted to the underside of

9.25 Dennis house. The grand southern space, looking toward the stair to the garage and caretaker's quarters. A peninsula of the upper eastern guest bedroom is at center right; the warm air recirculating tube is at center.

9.26 Dennis house.
The wall and gate to
the fountain court,
and the tile-edged
entry step.
(© Michael Jensen)

the roof; the vestibule is a glass-roofed peninsula analogous to those of the south exterior
wall. The eastern bedroom is a similar peninsula with a glass "roof," while its vestibule
comprises two such peninsulas. Each bedroom
is, to use Wendell Lovett's terminology, a self-
contained micro-cave-and-meadow. The
micro-cave, the northern two-thirds of each
bedroom, is all opacity, concrete solidity, dark
tones, wood and warmth. The southern third
of each room, the micro-meadow, is a white
and light peninsula with a view in three directions to the architectural supra-meadow, the
high southern volume—and thence to the

terraces and the valley beyond.

The closets and drawers of the vestibules
are gloriously crafted. Hygienic needs are
answered in bathrooms whose quite ordinary
fixtures are extraordinarily supported, anchored, trimmed, lit, housed, and accessoried.

The Garage and Studio

At the far eastern end of the southern sunlit
space a half-flight stair accesses the tennis
court and the garage. A further stair leads to
the caretaker's studio apartment above. The
architecture of all of these spaces, including the
garage, is similar to that of the bedrooms,

dining, and kitchen.

The Exterior Terraces, the Pool, and the Fountain

The exterior concrete work is as remarkable as that of the interior. Tile strips pervade all terrace surfaces. Wall surfaces are sandblasted except for a band at the edges, a detail that recalls the "drafted margins" of the finest classical Greek stonework. The large court-yard south of the helical-stair peninsula is edged by water. One enters through a wrought-iron gate, and across a channel of water by means of a tile-edged step, to find the water source against the southern wall. The fountain was inspired by one in England. Its craftsmen, British Engineering, of Hove, were commissioned to do this revised example; they did the fabrication in England and came to Sun Valley to supervise the assembly.

Terrace balustrades are of concrete, also with "drafted margins." The white disks in the squares at the end of each run are lights, and the undersides of the balustrades house downlighting.

The Dennis House: Some Closing Observations

The juxtaposition of high-tech and handcraft in this house has been noted elsewhere, and in one case at least has been said to be unre-solved.[9] But that is not the impression one has in the context of the building itself. The absence of any definable boundary between high-tech and handcraft, and the continual presence of both within any possible cone of vision, leave the impression of an entirely convincing integration of complementary realms. Technically and aesthetically this is a remarkable achievement.

The differences between the Dennis house and the Villa Simonyi are so great as to seem all-encompassing, and so obvious as to need no enumerating. And yet, considered experien-

tially, similarities between the two houses abound; or perhaps one should say that the degree to which Bystrom's composition illustrates Lovett's thought and his work in a larger sense is striking. The great southern space of the Dennis house encompasses all primary circulation both horizontal and vertical; it epitomizes what Lovett, in his work, has called a "go" space. But the upper and lower living rooms, the peninsulas for the TV and hot tub, and the breakfast alcove—Peggy Dennis's favorite spot—are equally clearly "stop" spaces, places of repose, quiet eddies along the river of light and space and move-ment. Or perhaps these peninsulas should be called clearings, because the space they complement is, throughout its considerable

9.27 *Dennis house. The fountain. Water drops onto the large wheel from the scupper at the end of the horizontal tube; the wheel then drives the sequence of subordinate reciprocating parts.*

extent, an architectural meadow as well—large, brightly lit, with extensive views to the exterior. The northern edge of this meadow is established by the dining and kitchen spaces, and the sleeping rooms on two levels. The lower of these rooms are micro-caves of unparalleled warmth; the upper ones are both dark micro-caves in their northern recesses, and bright micro-meadows to the south. And all these spaces look out to the larger meadow's glass wall, to the sequence of carefully scaled terraces, and to the landscape beyond.

Both Lovett and Wright have done compositions that can be similarly described, and Bystrom acknowledges an early debt to Lovett and the specific influence of Wright on this design.[10] Yet Bystrom's composition in no way declares either influence; it reveals how completely he has found his own way. It is an original and extraordinary accomplishment, technically, aesthetically, and experientially; no equally dramatic example in domestic architecture comes to mind.

Bystrom also acknowledges Wright's inspiration in the sense of shelter that is felt throughout the house, and is notably palpable in the northern rooms. It is worth noting, however, that even in his college days Bystrom had admired Aalto's work too, as an important complement to the severity of European modernism. In this connection it is interesting that Sigfried Giedion's evaluation of one of Aalto's masterpieces applies so well to the Dennis house: "In this house a rare thing has been achieved; the feeling of an uninterrupted flow of space throughout the house is never lost, and yet the feeling of intimacy is preserved, wherever you are."[11]

Bystrom has also referred to a litany of other influences ("the great roofs of China and Japan, the houses of the Swiss Alps, the mast-framed stave churches of Norway, and of course the residences of Greene and Greene") that recall the breadth of influences Lionel Pries encouraged his students to consider.

Of Bystrom's citations, Greene and Greene particularly deserve a few remarks. In the early twentieth century the brothers Charles and Henry Greene built a series of houses in Southern California that revel in the use of wood. Each square inch of their designs—and many of their houses are large indeed—is hand finished, to exacting tolerances and often to a subtly elegant nonlinear

9.28 Dennis house. The westernmost terrace, on an October afternoon. (© Michael Jensen)

geometry, with edges softened or cushioned to consistent profiles. Typically several species of wood are used—cedar, cherry, redwood, and teak are most common—each species serving a role for which it is particularly suited. The various pieces are joined by means of integral interlocking shapes, by wooden pegs and "keys," and, especially for structural elements, by handwrought iron bands that can be snugged up as the decades go by. The floors of the terraces that open from these rooms are of specially selected or custom-fired brick interspersed with stone, each piece typically hand-selected for location, and often laid to nonplanar configurations. Such an architecture is no longer possible. The wealthiest of clients could not now afford craftspersons who possess the skills and the tools, and for that reason few such tools and no such craftspersons now exist outside the rarefied world of handcrafted furniture. If they did, the wealthiest of clients could not now responsibly put before them the prodigal quantity of fine materials to which Greene and Greene's craftsmen bent their skills.

Nevertheless, the Dennis house offers extraordinary challenges for the present-day craftsman; the concrete formwork and troweling, for example, demand attention to tolerances entirely out of the range of any imaginable industry standard. Yet although Bystrom has stretched contemporary limitations, he has also designed within them, as he must. All wood cuts are planar, as are all surfaces except those of the columns, so the dressing and finishing of all surfaces are achievable by machine work, and there are innumerable instances of interchangeable parts. There are a lot of pegs, but they are cylindrical, not conical, so simple drills and dowels will serve. There are no hand-eased edges, no sensuous curves, no relieving niches to be individually matched to wrought iron connectors. Likewise Bystrom acknowledges

the scarcity and expense of fine and even ordinary woods, and the responsibility to use them with care. Even so, by any contemporary standard there is a lot of extraordinary wood in the Dennis house, and a lot of extraordinary craftsmanship. These observations, taken together, probably mean that, like the work of Greene and Greene, we will not see the like of the Dennis house again.

9.29 Dennis house. The northern breakfast terrace.

9.30 Dennis house.
Concrete in two
finishes, tile, and
several species of
wood. (© University
of Washington
Libraries, Special
Collections)

Consultants, Contractors, and Special Suppliers

Client	Reid and Peggy Dennis
Architect	Arne Bystrom Architect FAIA; John Sanford, Project Coordinator; Eric Thiel, Construction Coordinator; Richard Arthur, Jilie Kreigh, Bruce Hubbard, Klaus Bodenmueller, Larry Mortimer, Project Personnel
Snow Country Consultant	Ian Mackinlay FAIA
Mechanical Consultant	Ensar Group
Mechanical contractor	G & H Sheetmetal, Inc., Ketchum, Idaho
Landscape Architect	Murase Associates, Portland, Oregon
Structural Engineer	Darrold Bolton, P. E.

Electrical Engineer	Torgerson-Yingling Associates
General Contractor	Grabher Construction Inc., Sun Valley, Idaho
Concrete	Monroe Concrete Inc., Ketchum, Idaho
Ceramic tile	Woodland Park Tile, Seattle, Washing
Beams, columns, railings, stairs	Gammon Bros., Carey, Idaho
Dining Room Furniture	Evert Sodergren, Seattle
Cabinetwork	Boise Molding and Milling, Boise, Idaho
Wrought Iron Work	Byron's Welding, Inc., Hailey, Idaho
The Fountain	British Engineering, Hove, England

9.31 Dennis house.
From the west.

*Arne Bystrom and
Wendell Lovett,
2004.*

A Perspective

As we have seen, Bystrom and Lovett began their architectural lives when European modernism was ubiquitous in the profession and was convincingly presented in most American schools, including MIT and, after 1948, the University of Washington. Both architects were thus offered, in their formative years, a clarity of design theory that would not be common to a later generation. That clarity seems to have been a particularly useful foundation for their growth. Similarly it may be fortunate that both architects have realized their professional lives in a far corner of the United States, which has given them some geographic, intellectual, and emotional distance from the intense polemics of subsequent decades. Thus these architects have been able to attend with unusual consistency the fundamental sources of architecture that modernism restated: the building's spatial configuration and organization, its constructional materials and methods of fabrication, and its structural system—all of these to be derived from the building's own time, place, and programmatic purpose. Consistent attention to these sources alone, however, would ultimately have yielded a repetitive and sterile career. Fortunately Bystrom and Lovett have had other sources of professional growth.

Both architects have drawn from the heritage of their childhood and adolescent experiences—with mechanistic things, with wooden things, with physics and mathematics, with music, with art. Both have spent their lives in a region remarkable for its gentle climate, its dramatic topography, its multitudinous expanses of salt and fresh water, its extensive and complex shores, and its lush and varied vegetation. Lovett and Bystrom have designed for some of its most extraordinary sites, and the opportunities and limitations of those sites have shaped and inspired their work.

We might note too that in the earliest years of their architectural lives both men encountered an unusual breadth of viewpoints. Lovett learned of European modernism in his undergraduate college years, through classroom and studio discourse and his discovery of Le Corbusier, but we must suppose that he learned something of Aalto as well. For he was accepted by Harvard's Graduate School of Design, at that time headed by Gropius, the former director of the Bauhaus and a central figure of European modernism. Yet Lovett chose MIT and Aalto, who exemplified a less centrist but far more inclusive philosophy. Lovett then, ostensibly rejecting much of Aalto's viewpoint, brought an intense European modernist epistle back to Washington. But again one must suppose that he brought something of Aalto's perspective too, for Bystrom seems to have heard from Lovett both messages. Bystrom's reference to the "cold-blooded" aspect of "the Bauhaus movement" suggests his readiness to hear of architects such as Aalto and the Saarinens—a readiness perhaps related to his own Scandinavian ancestry—while through his own initiative he studied Wright's beliefs and buildings. And both Lovett and Bystrom were introduced to the uniquely catholic eclecticism of Lionel Pries, which must have instilled, or encouraged, their own receptivity to a wide range of influences.

From their college days, then, both Bystrom and Lovett knew the words and the work of several modernists who believed that architecture must come from the problem itself, and from contemporary materials and methods, but also believed that it must address a broad range of other considerations. To that foundation, in ensuing years, Bystrom and Lovett added their own continuing growth experiences.

Lovett, after graduation from MIT, found in Fred Bassetti a wealth of ideas and encouragement, and through *Domus* kept abreast of a wide range of significant Italian work. Twelve years later he experienced an epiphany at Stuttgart, and in the consequent remodeling of his Hilltop house he took his first steps on the path toward his own architecture. Bystrom, four years after graduation, had his Grand Tour, and found in the medieval buildings of France something he was seeking, and perhaps more than what he thought he was seeking. Shortly thereafter, while employed by Paul Thiry, he made an equally memorable pilgrimage to Wright's Fallingwater and Johnson's Wax. Twelve years later, in the prototypical restaurants for Stuart Anderson and the bathhouse projects, Bystrom too began to define his own direction.

In subsequent decades, Lovett's understanding of structure as an informing source has been enriched by his study of the work of Maillart and Calatrava and, at a smaller scale, by his many decades of familiarity with Italian design innovation. He continues to explore the joy of a closely related high-tech craft expressionism. And he has continued his cognitive study of intuition and emotion, in the writings of Carl Jung and in the work of more recent researchers and theorists on human emotion and architectural space. Bystrom's broadened influences include the work of Greene and Greene, the ancient architecture of China and

Japan, and the Norwegian stave church. His adaptation of stave-church structure may seem to contravene the modernist mandate that the building must be of its own time and place; yet his adaptation, in its actual usage, is not inconsistent with its time, and is intimately of its place. And in every case Bystrom's structures are informed by his intuitive and cognitive grasp of physics, and are invariably organized with a mathematician's geometric clarity. He continues to find a fundamental emotional sustenance in the material, common to all these influences, from which he has loved to make things all of his life.

Lovett's interest in human emotions and anthropomorphic forms, Bystrom's love of wood, and the dedication of both architects to crafted detail, are particularly appropriate to smaller buildings, and perhaps homes above all. It is understandable that many in the Puget Sound area who sought architects for their homes would turn to these men, and that their careers should thrive on that building type. But many architects who begin at that scale, and with that building type, find that success invites—almost demands—larger commissions and a larger staff, and as the scale of their work changes, so, perhaps, does their relationship to it. Aalto and Wright were notable exceptions to this generalization, and it is our good fortune that Lovett and Bystrom, like their respective role models, have spent the better part of their careers designing those smaller buildings to which their abilities and affections are so well suited.

Finally, the most important of their sources of growth lies outside the realm of cognitive inquiry. For both Lovett and Bystrom have evinced, from some indeterminate early point in life, what Gilbert Eade describes as an "innate ability" that "draws forth some intangible subconscious realization, and, through a rare compositional skill we call creativity, gives that realization a tangible form that brings us pleasure."

In these early years of the twenty-first century, after many intervening polemics, we find that our prevalent architecture is once again a manifestation of basic modernist tenets. It is also something more, and in ways that resonate with the work of Lovett and Bystrom. The acceptable forms that may now derive from materials, methods, and purposes are far more free, less dogmatically prescribed, not just in the work of a few but on a widespread basis. And that list of determinants—materials, methods, and purposes—is no longer sufficient to describe the issues that legitimately inform design. Monumentality is again a respectable word. The region and, more narrowly, the site, are studied not just for their apparent physical characteristics—contour lines, prevailing winds, and sun angles—but also for their ecological and cultural dimensions. History is again a legitimate contributor, not as the text from which the École des Beaux-Arts drew its lessons, nor as the superficial applique it so often became in Postmodernist usage, but as formal and cultural material that can provide greater depth and meaning, even inspiration. And our growing knowledge of the human mind is deepening our understanding of our emotional responses to architectural forms and spaces. In these ways modernism, once all but discarded as a creative design foundation, has entered a new and thriving phase.

Lovett and Bystrom are a part of this story, but their place in it is unusual. Their concision of practice and project, and their undistracted attention to shared principles, have allowed them to enjoy, in their different ways, a rare and remarkably focused five decades of growth. From innate abilities and seized opportunities, they have produced an evolving array of projects that have cast their

individual impress on modernist sources of architectural form and space. Their work is a distinguished part of a newly thriving modernism; it can also be seen to have been in the vanguard.

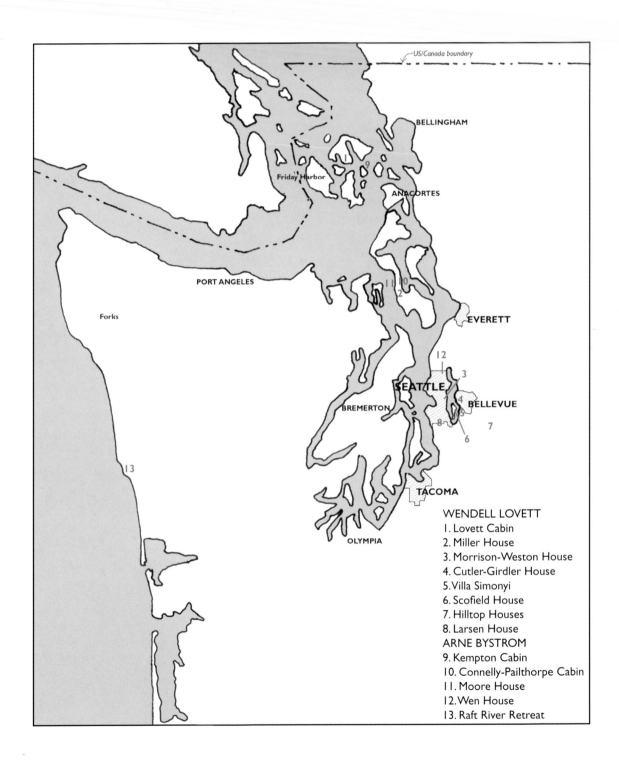

US/Canada boundary

BELLINGHAM

Friday Harbor

ANACORTES

PORT ANGELES

Forks

EVERETT

SEATTLE

BELLEVUE

BREMERTON

TACOMA

OLYMPIA

WENDELL LOVETT
1. Lovett Cabin
2. Miller House
3. Morrison-Weston House
4. Cutler-Girdler House
5. Villa Simonyi
6. Scofield House
7. Hilltop Houses
8. Larsen House
ARNE BYSTROM
9. Kempton Cabin
10. Connelly-Pailthorpe Cabin
11. Moore House
12. Wen House
13. Raft River Retreat

Appendix

Chronological Biographies of Wendell Lovett and Arne Bystrom, including Curricula Vitae and Complete Works

As of this writing, Lovett's drawings and documents are retained in his professional office. Bystrom's drawings and documents are in part retained in his office and in part archived in the Northwest Collection of the University of Washington Libraries, where they are accessible by a database.

Dates given for projects are for the year in which design was undertaken; in many cases, design and construction encompass several calendar years. Publications and awards associated with specific projects are listed with those projects; others are noted according to date of publication or conferral of award. All addresses and locations cited are in the state of Washington unless otherwise noted.

The AIA Seattle Medal, awarded to Lovett in 1993 and to Bystrom in 1998, is the highest honor the Chapter can confer; it is awarded, on no prescribed schedule, for a lifetime of distinguished achievement.

Wendell Harper Lovett

1922

April 2: born to Wallace and Pearl Harper Lovett, Seattle.

1947

Received Bachelor of Architecture degree, University of Washington, with AIA Student Silver Medal for excellence in design.
Married Eileen Whitson.
Enrolled in Master of Architecture program, Massachusetts Institute of Technology.

1948

Employed by Rapson, Demars, and Kennedy, Cambridge, Massachusetts.
Received Master of Architecture degree at MIT, with William R. Ware Prize.
Licensed as Architect, State of Washington, #475.
Began employment with Bassetti and Morse, Architects, Seattle.
Appointed Assistant Professor, Department of Architecture, University of Washington.

1949
Design

U.S. Junior Chamber of Commerce Competition, War Memorial Headquarters Offices.

Publication

U.S. Junior Chamber of Commerce Competition, *Progressive Architecture* (September 1949): 54.

Honors and Awards

Second Prize, *Progressive Architecture* and U.S. Junior Chamber of Commerce.

1950

Design

J. S. deBruder house, 3715 W Dravus Street, Seattle.

W. C. McConahan house, 3711 Kenyon Street, Seattle.

1951

Design

Wendell Lovett house, 14445 SE 55th Street, Hilltop Community, Bellevue (extensively altered; see 1961).

Gamma Rho Apartments, 4400 Fremont Avenue North, Seattle (in association with Bassetti and Morse).

Publication

Wendell Lovett house in: "House in the Northwest," *Arts and Architecture* (June 1952): 28-29; *Interiors* (June 1953): 100-105; *Arts and Architecture* 70 (July 1953): 28-29; Victor Steinbrueck, *Seattle Architecture, 1850-1953* (New York: Reinhold, 1953): 51; N/A, *World's Contemporary Houses, USA*, iv (Tokyo: Shokoku-sha, 1954): 20-23; *l'Architecture d'Aujourd'hui* 52 (February 1954): 10-11; "Maison Economique," *l'Architecture d'Aujourd'hui* (October 1956): 23; "Casa de un Arquitecto," *Informes de la Construccion* (April 1957): 49; and Victor B. Scheffer, *Hilltop: A Collaborative Community* (Bellevue Historical Society, 1994): 14-16.

Gamma Rho house in Steinbrueck, *Seattle*: 41; *Progressive Architecture* (June 1953): 83-85; and *Architectural Record* (August 1953): 194-95.

Honors and Awards

For the Wendell Lovett house: The American Institute of Architects (hereafter AIA), Washington State Honor Award (1953).

Exhibitions

For the Wendell Lovett house: invited to show at the International Exhibition of Architecture, II Bienal, São Paulo, Brazil, Museum of Modern Art (1955).

1953

Design

Motel, Castle Rock.

1954

Appointed Associate Professor with tenure, Department of Architecture, University of Washington.

Design

Wallace Lovett house I, 12318 SE 23rd Street, Bellevue.

"Firehood" patented, licensed for manufacture by Condon-King Company.

Publication

Wallace Lovett house I in "The Year's Work: A House in Bellevue, Wa.," *Interiors* (August 1956): 87.

Furniture and fireplaces in: "Dr. David van Browne Residence," *Architectural Record* (April 1953): 177-78; "Prefabricated Fireplace Design," *Arts and Architecture* (March 1954): 17; "Prefabricated Firehood," *Architecture and Building* (February 1957): 83; "Upholstered Lounge Chair," *Domus* (February 1954): 58; "Camino per la Serie," *Domus* (June 1956): 18; and Roggio Aloi, *Esempi: Camini d'Oggi* (Rome: Ulrico Hoepli, 1957): 198-99, 246-47.

Exhibitions

For the Wallace Lovett house I: invited to show at the International Exhibition of Architecture, IV Bienal, São Paulo, Brazil, Museum of Modern Art (1959).

For the "Flexifibre," later "Bikini," chair: invited to show at the International Exhibition of Modern Decorative and Industrial Arts and Architecture, Decima Triennale di Milano (1954).

Honors and Awards

For Wallace Lovett house I: AIA Seattle Honor Award (1955).

For the "Flexifibre," later "Bikini," chair: International Award in Furniture Design, Decima Triennale di Milano (1954).

1955

Design

Gervais Reed house, 5264 148th Avenue SE, Bellevue.

Publication

Reed house in "Gervais Reed house," *Arts and Architecture* (December 1957): 28-29; "Il Camino nella Casa Moderna," *L'illustrazione Italiana* (January 1958): 49; "Experimental House," *Sunset* (January 1960): 70; "Casa sula Collina, ad est di Seattle," *Domus* (May 1960): 9-11; "For a Family of Four: An Aerodynamic Vacation House," *Interiors* (March 1962): 96-97; "Vivienda Unifamiliar," *Informes de la Construccion* (July 1962): 99; "Maison des Vacances aux Environs de Seattle," *l'Architecture d'Aujourd'hui* (September 1962): 96-97; Roberto Aloi, *Camini e Ambienti* (Rome: Ulrico Hoepli, 1963): 252-55, 266-68 (also includes Giovanelli house of 1957); and Karl Kaspar, *Vacation Houses, an International Survey* (New York: Praeger, 1967): 108-9.

Honors and Awards

For the Reed house: *Sunset*/AIA Western Home Award in Architecture for Experimental Design.

1957

Design

Mary Jane Worth house, 4218 NE 92nd Street, Seattle.

Wallace Lovett house II, 5051 Ivanhoe Place NE, Seattle.

Roy Mattern house, 5242 48th Avenue SE, Hilltop community, Bellevue.

Gordon Giovanelli house addition, Ferncroft Road, Mercer Island (demolished).

Publication

"Prize Winning Curtain Walls," *Architectural Forum* (June 1956): 161.

"Small House," *Arts and Architecture* (April 1956): 28-29.

Giovanelli house addition in:"Soggiorno sul lago," *Domus* (June 1957): 7; "Lakeside Pavilion Under a Winged Roof," *Interiors* (November 1957): 120-21; "Casa Gordon Giovanelli," *Informes de la Construccion* (April 1962): 161-69; and "Habitation de pres Seattle," *l'Architecture d'Aujourd'hui* (September 1962): 72-73.

Worth house in: *Sunset* (October 1961): 74-75; "House by Wendell Lovett, Architect," *Arts and Architecture* (April 1962): 16-17: and "Habitation près de Seattle," *l'Architecture d'Aujourd'hui* (September 1962): 67.

Wallace Lovett house II in Ernest Danz, *Sonnenschutz, Sun Protection* (Verlag Gerd Hatje, 1967): 122.

Honors and Awards

For the Worth house: *Sunset/* AIA Western Home Competition First Honor Award (1961).

For the Wallace Lovett house II: AIA Washington State Honor Award (1961).

1958

Design

Alpha Tau Omega fraternity house alterations, 1800 NE 47th Street, Seattle (in association with Gene Zema, Architect).

1959

Design

Gordon Giovanelli house, 4456 Ferncroft Road, Mercer Island.

Publication

Giovanelli house in: "Residential Details," *Progressive Architecture* (November 1960): 142-44; "Una Casa Sull'isola," *Domus* (June 1964): 34-41; and Oscar Neuman, *CIAM '59 in Otterlo* (Stuttgart, 1961): 48-52.

Awards

For the Giovanelli house: *Seattle Times*/AIA Seattle "Home of the Year" (1959).

Appointed Fulbright Lecturer at Technical Institute of Stuttgart (1959-60).

1960

Design

Nuclear Reactor Building, University of Washington, Seattle (in association with Daniel Streissguth and Gene Zema).

Publication

Nuclear Reactor Building in: "Technical Building by the Architect Artist Group," *Arts and Architecture* (September 1959): 25; "Strong Lines Lead Students to Nuclear Learning," Architecture West (December 1962): 18-19; "Nuclear Reactor Building," *Arts and Architecture* (January 1963): 22-23; "A Teaching Reactor in a Glass Pavilion," *Architectural Record* (September 1963): 182-83; and "Réacteur Nucléaire de l'Universite de Washington à Seattle," *l'Architecture d'Aujourd'hui* (September 1965): lix.

Exhibitions and Lectures

Four invited lectures: Amerika Haus, Tubingen, Germany.

Invited Lecture: "Problems of the Urban Environment," U.S. Cultural Center, Paris.

1961

Design

Toronto City Hall Competition (in association with Daniel Streissguth and Gene Zema).

Pedestrian walkway shelters for Century 21 (in association with Ted Bower, Architect).

Wendell Lovett house, "Hilltop," remodeled, 14445 SE 55th Street, Bellevue.

Publication

Hilltop remodeling in" "Remodeling for Today," *American Home* (September 1966): 54-55; "Wendell H. Lovett Home and Studio," *Architecture West* (April 1968): 26-27; and Toshi Jukatu, *Architects' Own Houses of the World* (Tokyo: Edita, 1983): 128-33.

Honors and Awards

For the Hilltop remodeling: AIA Seattle Honor Award (1965).

1962

Design

Sidney Gerber house, 3302 South Washington Street, Seattle.

1964

Design

William Telford house addition, Mercer Island (demolished).

AIA National Headquarters Competition, Washington, D.C.

1965

Appointed Full Professor, Department of Architecture, University of Washington.

Design

Sullivan, Redman, and Winsor law offices, Smith Tower, Seattle (demolished).

Gordon Black house addition, 14841 SE 54th Street, Bellevue.

MacDonald, Hoge, and Bayless law offices, Hoge Building, Seattle.

1966

Design

John B. Crosetto, Jr., house addition, 14809 SE 54th Street, Bellevue.

Kerr, McCord, and Moen law offices, Hoge Building, Seattle.

Lycette, Diamond, and Sylvester office lobby, Hoge Building, Seattle.

Peter Meilleur house, 238 171st Place NE, Bellevue.

"Toetoaster" fireplace patented.

Publication

Meilleur house in: *Record Houses 1969 (Architectural Record,* mid-May 1969): 74-75; Jeremy Robinson, ed., *Affordable Houses* (New York: McGraw-Hill, 1979): 98-99 (also contains Crane Island retreat, 44-45); and Harry Martin and Dick Busher, *Contemporary Homes of the Pacific Northwest* (Seattle: Madrona, 1980): 130-35.

"Toetoaster" in Menges Hatje, *Modern Fireplaces* (New York: Architectural Book Publishing Company, 1979): 6, 46-47, 49-50, 58-59, 132-33.

1967
Design
Nicholas Podvorac house, 9726 49th Avenue NE, Seattle.

1968
Design
New AIA Seattle offices, Occidental Avenue, Seattle (demolished).
Jack Melill house, 7446 92nd Avenue SE, Mercer Island.
Publication
AIA offices in: "Refurbished with a Flourish: Offices Seattle Chapter AIA," *Architecture West* (July 1969): 114-15; and "AIA Chapter Offices, Seattle, Washington," *Architectural Record* (January 1973): 99.
Melill house in: "The Pleasure is in the Strong Discipline of Form and Detail," *Sunset* (October 1969): 96; Ella Moody, ed., *Decorative Art in Modern Interiors* (London: Studio Vista, 1970): 50-51; "Jack Melill House by Wendell Lovett," *Architecture and Urbanism*, (Tokyo) (February 1971): 67-70; and "A Design Tailored to the Trees," *American Home* (March 1971): 66-69.
Honors and Awards
For the Melill house: *Sunset*/AIA Western Homes Competition Merit Award (1970).
For the AIA Offices; *Architectural Record* National Award of Excellence for Interior Design (1973).

1969
Design
Dr. Cecil K. Stedman house, New Denver, British Columbia, Canada.
Lauren Studebaker house, 7545 East Mercer Way, Mercer Island (altered).
Publication
Studebaker house in: "Studebaker House," *Architecture and Urbanism* (Tokyo) (July 1971): 15-20; "A House That Says Welcome," *American Home* (November 1971): 98-99; *Record Houses of 1972* (Architectural Record, mid-May 1972): 54-57; "La Maison Studebaker en Seattle," *Informes de la Construccion* (November 1972): 11-16; "Studebaker House," *L'architectura* (December 1972): 528-29; and "Space," *House Beautiful's Building Manual* (Spring/Summer 1973): 125-28.
Honors and Awards
For the Studebaker house: *Seattle Times*/AIA Seattle "Home of the Year," 1971; Burlington Award for Residential Interiors (1971); and *Architectural Record* National Award of Excellence in Residential Design (1971).

1970
Design
Lovett vacation retreat, Crane Island.

W. Prescott Miller house, Panorama Road, Whidbey Island.

David Munday vacation house, Crystal Mountain.

Publication

Lovett retreat in: "Lovett Vacation House," *Architecture and Urbanism,* (Tokyo) (February 1971): 67-70; "The Perfect Escape," *Architectural Forum* (September 1971): 7; "Sunny Deck House," *American Home* (June 1972): 60-61; "Dal Mare: quasi invisibile tra gli alberi," *Domus* (October 1972): 7; "En helt anden slags feriehus," *Bo Bedre,* (Copenhagen) (July 1973): 36-39; "Carefree and Adaptable," *Better Homes and Gardens Building Ideas* (Fall-Winter 1973): 73-75; "Weekend-Holzhaus Zwishen Wasser und Wald," *Bauen und Wohnen* (Zurich) (December 1973): 504; *Record Houses of 1974* (Architectural Record, mid-May 1974): 86-87; "Kontrast zu den 4 Wanden daheim, Ferienhus auf San Juan, USA," *Architektur und Wohnwelt* (Stuttgart) (July 1974): 294-95; and *Architectural Record*, ed., *Vacation Houses* (New York: McGraw-Hill, 1997): 216-19.

Miller house in: "Miller house," *Architecture and Urbanism* (Tokyo) (November 1972): 92-93.

Munday house in "Basic and Functional: A Lodge-like Snow House," *House and Garden Second House* (Fall-Winter 1974-75).

Honors and Awards

For the Lovett retreat: *Sunset*/AIA Western Homes Competition Merit Award (1971); American Plywood Association National Citation in Architecture (1972); and *Architectural Record* National Award of Excellence for House Design (1974).

1971

Design

Robert Coppernoll house, 2504 West Lake Sammamish Road SE, Bellevue.

1972

Design

Gerald Frey house, 4526 132nd Avenue NE, Bellevue.

Mary Jane Potter house addition, 4218 East 92nd Street, Seattle.

Kim Simonelli house, 72nd Avenue NE, Kirkland.

Publication

Frey house in: "Frey House, Bellevue, Wa.," M. Uyeda, ed., *Global Architecture Houses #2* (Tokyo: Edita, 1972): 38-43; "Una Casa nel verde," *Domus* (November 1973); 9-12; "Frey House," *A+U* (Tokyo) (March 1974): 33-48; and Mario Schofield, ed., *Decorative Art and Modern Interiors* (London: Studio Vista, 1975): 98-105.

Honors and Awards

For the Frey house; AIA Seattle Honor Award (1973).

1973

Design

William Wallace house, 5003 East Mercer Way, Mercer Island.

Publication

Wallace house in: " *A+U* (Tokyo) (April 1974): 27-34.

1974

Design

John Leslie house, Blakeley Island.

Ward Swift vacation house, Link Island.

Spencer Moseley addition, Seattle (not built).

1975

Design

Donald Grish house, 23212 SE 368th Street, Enumclaw.

Melvin Fujita house, 7220 94th Avenue SE, Mercer Island (altered).

Publication

Fujita house in: "A Spectacular House …" *House and Garden* (London) (September 1979): 116-19.

1976

Design

Max Scofield house, 5007 East Mercer Way, Mercer Island.

Publication

Scofield house in: M. Uyeda, ed., *Global Architecture Houses #3* (Tokyo: Edita, 1977): 176-81; Harry Martin, *Contemporary Homes of the Pacific Northwest* (Seattle: Madrona, 1980): 136-41; "Hail (and Farewell?) to the Northwest School," *Architecture Minnesota* (October/November 1981): 44-47; and Grant Hildebrand, *The Wright Space* (Seattle: University of Washington Press, 1991): 156-59.

Honors and Awards

For the Scofield house: AIA Seattle Merit Award (1978).

1977

Design

Dr. Paul Ballard house, 2302 NW Blue Ridge Drive, Seattle.

1978

Design

Erling Larsen house, 12919 69th Avenue South, Seattle.

Honors and Awards

Elected to College of Fellows of the AIA.

1979

Design

William Wahl house, 700 SE Shoreland Drive, Bellevue.

Larry Monson house, 4817 East Mercer Way, Mercer Island.

Publication

Monson house in: *Process Architecture* (May 1982): 152-55.

Honors and Awards

For the Wahl house: Seattle-King County Realtors Environmental Award.

1980
Design
Spinnaker West Apartments, Seattle (not built).

Juris Vagners and Linda Christianson house, 20745 Chief Sealth Drive NE, Miller Bay, Indianola.

Don Lysons house alterations, 14836 SE 54th Street, Hilltop Community, Bellevue.

Dick Peterson house, 4920 NE 87th Street, Seattle.

Publication
"Wendell Lovett, A Worldly Provincial," *The Weekly* (Seattle) (September 10, 1980): 16-18.

Peterson house in: *Process Architecture* (May 1982): 148-51.

1981
Design
Gerhardt Morrison and Julie Weston house, 416 34th Avenue, Seattle.

William Gillis house, Cougar Mountain, Issaquah.

Publication
"Hail (and Farewell?) to the Northwest School," and Larry Woodin, "Designer's Profile: Lovett Believes Buildings Make Gestures," *Architecture Minnesota* (October/November 1981): 44-47.

1982
Design
Dale Overfield house, 12525 35th Street East, Puyallup.

William Neukom house, 621 36th Avenue, Seattle.

1983
Design
Bob Hansen vacation house, Hyak.

Wendell Lovett house, 420 34th Avenue, Seattle.

1984
Design
San Cho house, 16519 35th Avenue NE, Seattle.

Gar LaSalle and Nina Ferrari house, SW Point Robinson Road, Maury Island.

1985
Design
Jerry Crosby house, 14407 SW Pohl Road, Vashon Island.

Eric Farley house, 18724 SE 65th Place, Cougar Mountain, Issaquah.

1986
Design
Anne Gould Hauberg condominium interior, 1223 Spring Street, Seattle (in association

with Alan Liddle, Architect).

Mark Hershman and Ted Rothstein vacation house, Decatur Island.

1987

Retired from full-time teaching; elected Professor Emeritus, Department of Architecture, University of Washington.

Design

Tim Proctor house, 11655 72nd Place NE, Kirkland.

Charles Simonyi house, Villa Simonyi (phase I), 111 84th Avenue NE, Medina.

Publication

Simonyi house in: "Geometry and Physics Meet Glass and Concrete," *New York Newsday Guide to Design and Decor* (September 27, 1992): 16, 17, 20; "The Villa Simonyi," *A+U* (Tokyo) (March 1993): 122-27; and "Hoch Hinaus," *Wohn!Design* (Stuttgart) (January/ February 1995): 68-77.

1988

Design

Boone Barker vacation house, Deer Harbor, Orcas Island.

Francois Dureau house, "Maison Dureau," North Scenic Heights Road, Whidbey Island (not built).

1989

Design

Peggy Goldman house, 2643 Perkins Lane, Seattle.

Honors and Awards

For the Simonyi house: AIA Seattle Commendation.

1990

Design

Bob Hansen house, 3 Lindley Road, Mercer Island.

1991

Design

Charles Simonyi condominium interior, Résidence les Oliviers, Monaco.

Brian Werthheimer condominium interior, 87 Virginia Street, Seattle.

1993

Design

David Hmiel and Christine Knowles vacation house, 17201 North Shore Road, Leavenworth.

Charles Simonyi house additions (phase II), 111 84th Avenue NE, Medina.

Publication

The Simonyi house additions in: "Seattle Reigns: Wendell Lovett," *Newsweek* (May 20, 1996): 52; "Swapping Options for Art," *Forbes* (December 2, 1996): 276, 278; "Vasarely's

Alphabet," *Spiegl, Wohnen 2000* (May 1997): 74-75; "Computer Driven," *Audio Visual Interiors* (June 1997); 50-64; "Villa Simonyi," *Revista Ed, estillo de vida y decoracion* (Santiago) (February 1997): 78-85; "Cyber Toy Story," *Newsweek* (August 4, 1997): 56-59; and "Technovision," *Custom Home* (May 2000): 56-61.

Honors and Awards

AIA Seattle Medal for distinguished lifetime achievement in architecture, in design and design education.

1994

Design

Eric Farley house addition, 18724 SE 65th Place, Cougar Mountain, Issaquah.

1997

Design

David Cutler and Debrah Girdler house, 609 Evergreen Point Road, Medina.

Honors and Awards

For the Cutler-Girdler house: AIA Seattle Commendation.

1998

Publication

"Alvar Aalto/Wendell Lovett," *Arcade, the Northwest Journal for Architecture and Design* (Winter 1998): 34-35.

1999

Design

Juris Vagners and Linda Christianson house, 16376 North Shore Road, Leavenworth.
Charles Simonyi house additions (phases III and IV), 111 84th Avenue NE, Medina.

2001

Design

Raul Meilleur and Tracy Buren house, Preston.

2002

Design

Jack Johnson house, Burien.
Jerry Leigh house, North Lake Wenatchee Shore Road, Leavenworth.

Employees

Stewart Arentzen	Clayton Evans	Drew Rocker
Suzanne Ritus	Rob Henry	Gareth Shuh
Elise Ching	Keith Howell	Gordon Walker
Susana Covarrubias	John Kolmodin	Mark Whetstone
Reider Dittman	Joanne Krippaehne	Associate
Donald Doman	John Majewski	Charles J. Williams III
Maude Entoft	Neil Middleton	

Carl Arne Bystrom

1927

June 8: born to Albin and Martha Hammerose Bystrom, Seattle.

1951

Received Bachelor of Architecture degree, summa cum laude, University of Washington, with AIA Student Silver Medal for excellence in design.
Licensed as Architect, State of Washington, #619.
Began employment with Seidelhuber Iron and Bronze Works, Seattle.

1953

Toured Europe, especially Italy and France.
Began employment with Paul Thiry, Architect.
Design
Howard Whittlesley house, 5307 SW Pritchard Street, Seattle.

1955
Design
E. C. Grubbe house, 1142 North 77th Street, Seattle.

1957

Began employment with Decker and Christiansen, Architects.

1958

Founded Bystrom and Greco, Architects, with partner James Greco.
Design
Carsten Lien house, 8010 40th Avenue NE, Seattle.
Paul F. McAllister house, 9330 Sunset Way, Bellevue (not built).
Honors and Awards
For the Lien house: *Seattle Times*/AIA Seattle "Home of the Year."

1959

Appointed Assistant Professor, Department of Architecture, University of Washington.
Design
Michael Adams house, 78th Place NE, Medina.
F. Deckebach house, 153rd Avenue SE, Mercer Island.
Howard Miller house addition, 4848 East Mercer Way, Mercer Island.
Sand Point Country Club, 8333 55th Avenue NE, Seattle.
Dr. K. M. Robertson clinic, 20th Street NW, Oak Harbor.
Overlake Plymouth showroom, 116th Avenue NE, Bellevue (not built).
French Quarter Cafe, for Stuart Anderson, 1326 7th Avenue, Seattle (demolished).
H. P. White Apartments, 11th Avenue East at East John Street, Seattle.
Frank Anderson house, 56th Place NE at 56th Street NE, Seattle.

Everett Elks Club remodeling, 2731 Rucker Avenue, Everett.

Publication

Miller house in: "They Simply Built a New Upstairs," *Sunset* (October 1963): 99.

Sand Point Country Club in: *Architecture West* (September 1963): 24-25.

Robertson Clinic in: *Architectural Record* (June 1959): 191; and *Deutsche Bauzeitschrift* (November 1964): 177-78.

Honors and Awards

For the Miller house: *Sunset*/AIA Western Home Competition Award.

1960

Married Valerie Broze.

Design

Albin Bystrom house, 3811 56th Avenue SW, Seattle.

Robert Zech house, 8101 SE 48th Street, Mercer Island.

Jerome Zech cabin, Whidbey Island.

Tordal Dannevig house, 5112 145th Place SE, Bellevue.

Publication

Zech house in: "Awards of Merit," *Sunset* (October 1961): 71; and *Interiors* (March 1963).

Honors and Awards

For the Zech house: *Sunset*/AIA Western Home Competition Award.

1961

Resigned Assistant Professorship, University of Washington.

Design

Builders' Brick showroom, scheme I, 3720 Airport Way South, Seattle (not built).

Frank Verginia house, 2721 60th SE, Mercer Island.

Ralph Umbarger house, Maltby Road, Snohomish.

Gold Coast Restaurant in the Frye Hotel, for Stuart Anderson, 223 Yesler Way, Seattle (demolished).

1962

Design

Jones Apartments, scheme I: West Lee Street at 7th Avenue, scheme II: 3600 25th Avenue West, Seattle.

Kesgard Apartments, 14th Avenue West at West Barrett Street, Seattle.

Builders' Brick-Mutual Materials showroom, scheme II, 3720 Airport Way South, Seattle.

Publication

Jones Apartments, scheme I in: *Architecture West* (August 1963): 32.

Builders Brick-Mutual Materials in: "News Report," *Progressive Architecture* (June 1963): 58.

Honors and Awards

For Builders Brick-Mutual Materials: AIA Seattle Citation for architectural graphics.

1963

Elected to the Board of Allied Arts of Seattle.

Design

Remodeling for new offices of Bystrom and Greco, 761 Bellevue Avenue East, Seattle.

School of Librarianship alterations, University of Washington, Seattle.

Century Building, 10 Harrison Street, Seattle.

Publication

Century Building in: "Where Architects Hang Their Hats," *AIA Journal* (October 1964): cover and 33; and "News Report," *Progressive Architecture* (October 1964): 102.

School of Librarianship in: *Journal of Education for Librarianship* (Summer 1964): 45-52.

Honors and Awards

For the Century Building: Prestressed Concrete Institute Award.

1964

Bystrom and Greco relocate to the Century Building.

1965

Design

James Tuttle house, 5109 West Hanford Street, Seattle.

J. P. Jones house, 40th Avenue East, Seattle.

James W. Whittaker house remodeling, 2434 West Lake Sammamish Boulevard, Bellevue.

1967

Design

Delta Chi fraternity addition, 1819 NE 47th Street, Seattle.

Angus Buchanan house remodeling, 538 West Lake Sammamish Boulevard, Bellevue.

Hagen Apartments, Seattle (not built).

1968

Design

Forward Thrust projects for the City of Seattle: remodeling of Seward Park Bathhouse to Seward Park Cultural Center; Greenlake Bathhouse to Bathhouse Theater; and Madrona Bathhouse to Madrona Dance Studio.

"Black Angus" restaurants for Elliott Bay, Seattle; Bellevue; and Tacoma.

"Tiki Hut" for Ruff Enterprises, Lynnwood.

Henry Art Gallery remodeling, University of Washington.

Honors and Awards

For the Bathhouses: Seattle/King County Realtors Environmental Design Award.

1969

Design

North Acres Park restrooms, 12718 1st Avenue NE, Seattle.

1970

Design

Blue Six Condominiums, Warm Springs Road, Ketchum, Idaho.

Arne Bystrom house remodeling, 1020 Summit Avenue East, Seattle.

The Bystrom cabin, Raft River on the Pacific Coast.

Sound Elevator Co. Inc. offices, 921 Elliott Avenue West, Seattle.

Publication

Bystrom cabin in: "A Tiny Cabin Thoreau Might have Built," *AIA Journal* (New American Architecture 1979): 178-80; "Working With Nature, Perched Above the Sea," *House and Garden Building and Remodeling Guide* (January/February 1981): 66-69: and Duo Dickenson, ed., *The Small House* (New York: McGraw-Hill, 1986): 112-15.

Bystrom house remodeling in: "Storage Around the Refrigerator," *Sunset* (October 1980): 130; and "Adding Verve to a Tired Victorian," *Historic Preservation* (April 1987): cover and 40-45.

Honors and Awards

For the Bystrom cabin: National AIA First Honor Award; *Sunset*/AIA Western Home Award; National AIA/*Housing* First Honor Award; and Red Cedar and Handsplit Shake Bureau Award.

1971

Design

"Black Angus" restaurants for San Mateo, California, and Spokane.

Stuart Anderson Ranch House, Thorpe.

Master plan and architectural design competition for Mercer Island Park District.

1972

Founding member of the Pike Place Market Historical Commission.

Design

Colman Pool (City of Seattle) alterations, Seattle.

1973

Design

"Stuart's" (restaurant), 6135 Seaview Avenue NW, Seattle.

Stuart Anderson Black Angus Restaurants Corporate Offices, 200 2nd Avenue West, Seattle.

Two "Black Angus" restaurants for unspecified locations.

Jack Simpson Condominiums, Warm Springs Ranch, Ketchum, Idaho.

1974

Licensed as Architect: State of Arizona, #9875; and State of California, #8164.

Design

Soames-Dunn Building alterations, Pike Place Market, Seattle (the first renovation in the Pike Place Market Historic District).

Honors and Awards

For the Soames-Dunn Building; U.S. Department of Housing and Urban Development Special Mention.

1975

Licensed as Architect: State of Alaska, #3850A; and State of Oregon, #1653.

1976

Design

"Straw Hat Pizza" prototype design; examples built in three sites in Seattle.

1977

Arne Bystrom Architect's office relocated to 1617 Post Alley, Pike Place Market, Seattle.

Design

Arne Bystrom Architect's office, 1617 Post Alley, Pike Place Market, Seattle.

Richard Peterson house, 1013 Evergreen Point Road, Medina.

Al Gosset house (not built).

Peggi Moore house, 5440 Grigware Road, Freeland, Whidbey Island.

Publication

Moore house in: "1981-1982 Western House Awards," *Sunset* (October 1981): cover and 75-77; *Record Houses of 1980* (*Architectural Record*, mid-May 1980): 102-3; "Hail (and Farewell?) to the Northwest School," *Architecture Minnesota* (October/November 1981): 36-40; "AIA Component Awards," *AIA Journal* (May 1981): 330; *Construction Times* (March 1982): cover; and "Forest Retreat on Whidbey Island," *Sun Coast Architect/Builder* (March 1983): cover and 26-27.

Peterson house in: "Richard Peterson House," *A+E* (1982): 56-59; and "Peterson House," *Process Architecture* (May 1982): 148-51.

Honors and Awards

For the Moore house: AIA Seattle Honor Award; *Sunset*/AIA Western Home Award; *Architectural Record* "Record House Award"; and Red Cedar and Handsplit Shake Bureau/AIA First Award.

1978

Design

Howard Richards house, Sun Valley, Idaho (not built).

Seattle Garden Center alterations, Pike Place Market, Seattle.

Sound Elevator Building, 9221 Elliott Avenue West, Seattle.

Diane Mason house, 2209 East Howe Street, Seattle.

1000 Trails, La Conner.

Publication

Seattle Garden Center in: "Up on the Roof," *Architectural Record* (April 1983): 150-51; and W. Shopsin, ed., *Restoring Old Buildings for Contemporary Uses* (New York: Whitney, 1986): 88-91.

1979

Design

David Ray house (not built).

1000 Trails, Bend, Oregon.

Heine Sorenson house, 7220 151st Street SW, Edmonds (not built).

James Lee house, 715 NW St. Helens Road, Smokey Point, Chehalis.

King County housing, Auburn.

Publication

Lee house in: "A Staircase of Lights," *House Beautiful Building Manual* (Spring-Summer 1984): 43-46.

1980

Design

Rodgers Block in Pike Place Market, schematic design.

Hiawatha Park Fieldhouse remodeling for Seattle Parks Department.

1981

Design

David Munday house, Eagle Nest at La Conner (not built).

1982

Design

Reid Dennis house and furnishings, 709 Fairway Drive, Sun Valley, Idaho.

Volunteer Park Conservancy Restoration Master Plan for Seattle Parks, Seattle.

Dianne Mason-Broze house alterations, 2209 East Howe Street, Seattle.

Publication

"Architecture Demystified," *Architecture Minnesota* (May 1982): 34-37.

Dennis house in: "Sun Valley House," *Progressive Architecture* (January 1985): 128-30; "P/A Awards Update," *Progressive Architecture* (January 1986): 149; "Ultimate Techno Home," *Popular Science* (August 1986): cover and 60-63; "A Marriage of Disciplines," *Progressive Architecture* (April 1987): 86-95; "Highly Crafted ... and Highly Technical," *Sunset* (October 1987): 72-73; E. Albert and T. Humphrey, eds., *The Northwest* (New York: Bantam, 1989): 200-213; "How Good Is the Wood?" *Architectural Record* (December 1990): 39; "Arne Bystrom Sun Valley House," Wayne N. T. Fujii, ed., *GA Houses 21* (Tokyo: Edita, 1987): 64-73; and Grant Hildebrand, *Origins of Architectural Pleasure* (Berkeley: University of California Press, 1999): 129-31.

Honors and Awards

For the Dennis house: National AIA Honor Award; *Progressive Architecture* Design Citation; *Sunset*/AIA Western Home Award; AIA Seattle Award of Merit; U.S. Department of Energy Award for Innovation.

City of Seattle Certificate of Merit for Outstanding Service.

1983

President, AIA Seattle.

Design

Bobby Kelly house, Bothell (not built).

Honors and Awards

Seattle Landmarks Preservation Board Certificate for Outstanding Service.

Invited juror for Sunset/AIA Western Home Awards.

1984

Honors and Awards

AIA Washington Council Commendation for Service to the Profession.

AIA Seattle Commendation for Service as President.

Invited juror for National AIA Honor Awards.

1985

Design

Robert Tsai and Mavis Kohlenberg house remodeling, 312 SW 292nd Street, Federal Way.

Honors and Awards

Elected to College of Fellows of the AIA.

AIA Certificate of Appreciation for Service to the Board of Directors.

Invited speaker and guest critic, California State University at San Luis Obispo.

1986

Design

Richard Fisher house alterations, Sun Valley, Idaho (not built).

William Krippaehne house, Glencove Point Road, Pierce County (not built).

David Lennartz house, 603 37th Avenue, Seattle.

Thom Dolder house remodeling (of a Paul Thiry design), 3410 East John Street, Seattle.

William Krippaehne house remodeling, 4870 NE 39th Street, Seattle.

Honors and Awards

Fellow of Northwest Institute of Architecture and Urban Studies in Italy.

Visiting lecturer, Rome Studies Program, University of Washington, Palazzo Pio, Rome.

Invited lecturer, Department of Architecture, Washington State University, Pullman.

Invited lecturer, Department of Architecture, University of Idaho, Moscow.

Visiting lecturer, Department of Architecture, Montana State University, Bozeman.

1987

Member, National AIA Design Committee.

1988

Member, National AIA Housing Committee.

President, Northwest Institute of Architecture and Urban Studies in Italy.

Honors and Awards

Visiting lecturer, Department of Architecture, University of Washington, Seattle.

Panelist, "Cutting Edge Colloquium," Evergreen State College, Olympia.

Visiting lecturer, Department of Architecture, Virginia Polytechnic and State University, Blacksburg, Virginia.

1989

Publication

"Northwest Style," *Arcade, the Northwest Journal for Architecture and Design* (October/ November 1989): 18.

1990

Design

James Kempton cabin, Obstruction Island, Jefferson County.

Publication

Kempton cabin in: "No Obstruction," *Progressive Architecture* (November 1992): 84-85.

Honors and Awards

Panelist, "Dilemmas in Design," AIA, Washington, D.C.

Domino's 50 Award for outstanding accomplishment in architecture.

1991

Design

Lynne Dunkley house, 10829 Bill Point Bluff NE, Bainbridge Island.

Frank Weinstein house, 482 39th Avenue East, Seattle (two projects, neither built).

1992

Design

Arne Bystrom garage and terrace, 1922 Summit Avenue East, Seattle.

Joel Connelly and Mickey Pailthorp cabin, Whidbey Island.

Publication

Connelly-Pailthorp cabin in: "A Tower in the Trees," *Sunset* (October 1995): 96-97; "Cabin Fever," *Seattle Magazine* (July 1996): 24-27; and Grant Hildebrand, *Origins of Architectural Pleasure* (Berkeley: University of California Press, 1999): 18-19.

Honors and Awards

For the Connelly-Pailthorp cabin: AIA Seattle Award of Merit; and *Sunset* Western Home Citation.

1993

Design

James Egbert house, 2707 Broadway Avenue East, Seattle (not built).

Robert Arnett house, 2499 deHaro Lane, San Juan Island (built without supervision).

Leroy Hood house, 6411 NE Windermere Road, Seattle.

Publication

Hood house in: "Natural Attraction," *Seattle Homes and Lifestyle* (February 1997): 42-47.

1994

Design

Michelle Pailthorp remodeling, 1422 35th Avenue, Seattle.

Iver Michelson house, 5510 298th Avenue SE, Preston.

1995
Design
Robert Chickman and Susan Lynette house, 790 Three Crabs Road, Sequim (preliminary drawings only).

1996
Design
John Burns house remodeling, 745 McGilvra Boulevard East, Seattle.

Bradford Edgerton house addition, 72313 83rd Avenue NE, Marysville (not built).

1997
Design
Thomas Reeve house, 5440 143rd Avenue SE, Bellevue.
Exhibitions
"To Dwell with Nature," at The Nordic Heritage Museum, Seattle, and Trondheim, Norway, curated by Are Oyasaeter.

1998
Design
Joseph Bolton house, Swan Road, Duvall (not built).
Honors and Awards
AIA Seattle Medal for distinguished lifetime achievement in architecture, in design and service to the profession.

2000
Design
Sudhaneelakantan Harinarayan house remodeling, 1722 Howell Place, Seattle.

Chris Carlson house, 16035 Inglewood Road NE, Kenmore (not built).

Ashish Gupta and Nita Goyal house remodeling, 3810 East McGilvra Street, Seattle.

2001
Design
"Seawhis" cabana, 4124 55th Avenue NE, Seattle.

Gary Hurlbut remodeling, 1409 Norcross Way, Seattle (not built).

2002
Design
"Seawhis" house, 4124 55th Avenue NE, Seattle.

2003
Design
W. F. Wilson house, Tract 5, Lot 4, Mason County.

Employees

Chris Andrejko
Robert Estep
Richard Floisand
Jan Fredrickson
An-Sofi Holst
Harvey Jaeger
Ron Jelaco
Craig Kasman

Louis Lakier
Ken MacInnes
Glen Nomura
Larry Porter
Philip Retz
John Sanford
Marietta Wilheim

Notes

Chapter 1: A Prologue

1. Walter Gropius, Le Corbusier, and, later, Erich Mendelssohn, claimed inspiration from American pragmatic technology, as manifested in the American factory and grain elevator especially. Gropius referred to his watershed 1911 Faguswerk at Alfeld as "an American factory," and Reyner Banham believed that Gropius had developed the design from photographs of Albert Kahn's Ford Highland Park plant in Detroit, completed in 1910, and Ernest Ransome's 1903 Beverley, Massachusetts factory for the United Shoe Machine Company, who were majority owners of Fagus. But Louis Sullivan, decades earlier, had worked from similar inspirations: "The Great Engineers were my heroes." Mumford, among others, has suggested that American architects, Wright included, were far in advance of Europe in integrating technology into design process and product, and that this may have freed them to turn their attention to a wider range of considerations. Mumford contrasts, for example, Le Corbusier's dramatization of the bare light bulb as a new-age icon, in about 1920, with Sullivan's convincing integration of it into the architecture of the Chicago Auditorium in 1889, or Wright's handling of electrical amenities in the Robie house and elsewhere by 1908.

Antonio Gaudi is clearly an exception to the portrayal of the Europeans as the technology-emphasis camp, but his work is so geographically circumscribed, and so personal, that it is hard to know how to place him in a concise synopsis.

2. Charles Moore's house for himself in Orinda, California, of 1961, included sliding barn doors and Tuscan columns—characteristics well outside any modernist canon. Five years later, Robert Venturi, in *Complexity and Contradiction in Architecture* (New York: Museum of Modern Art, 1966), advocated freedom from modernist dogma, arguing the value of historic reference, willfulness, and whimsy. And so, through the 1970s and 1980s, architecture embraced Postmodernism, Contextualism, New Classicism, and Deconstruction, in rapid succession. Each movement saw modernism as the villain; Robert A. M. Stern, in *Modern Classicism* (New York: Rizzoli, 1984), spoke of modernism's "short, nasty, and brutish existence." The harsher evaluations now seem simply wrongheaded. Modernism's obvious failings were addressed, as early as the 1940s, by Mumford and others. But few, then or now, would call the Villa Mairea, Fallingwater, the Lovell house, the Johnson's Wax buildings, the Villa Savoye, or the Barcelona Pavilion "nasty" or "brutish." And modernism's essential tenets still prevail. To cite as evidence the work of I. M. Pei, Fumihiko Maki, Aldo Giurgola, or Carlo Scarpa would invite the objection that they represent an insufficiently youthful generation; but that cannot be said of Mario Botta, Tadao Ando, Arata Isozaki, Glenn Murcutt, Steven Holl, or Santiago Calatrava.

3. With only the exception that two examples of Bystrom's prototypical restaurant design for Stuart Anderson's "Black Angus" chain were built in California.

Chapter 2: Wendell Lovett's Formative Years

1. Lovett has driven interesting cars throughout his adult life. At this writing he drives a yellow Porshe Boxster with rust-red interior. He had a poster of an Audi TT on his

office wall for several months; it was recently replaced by a profile view of a Bugatti Type 35.

2. Interview Lovett/Booth, October 2000.

3. Foremost of whom were Paul Hayden Kirk and Roland Terry, who both produced stunning work in school. Terry's work was often modernist or Moderne. Kirk's work, rather surprisingly, is typically a gorgeous mainfestation of the École des Beaux-Arts style. One of Kirk's projects in particular, entitled "A retreat for an American convert to Buddhism, in a mountainous setting, that is to serve as a monastery, and as a shrine for a gigantic statue of Buddha," was presented in one of the most extravagant École *analytiques* known, on two 40 by 60 inch sheets, in watercolor wash, with sectional cuts shown in a deep crimson. It is entirely possible that Lovett saw this project during his field trip. The work is in the Department's archives.

4. We are indebted to Jeffrey Karl Ochsner for bringing this exhibit to our attention.

5. American schools kept the École terminology along with the method. This may have been seen as prestigious, but it was also convenient, since there is no real English equivalents for many of the terms, including *en charrette,* not cited here but still in use. The term means, literally, on the cart (i.e., the cart sent around the studio when projects were due); drawings not on the cart were not accepted. The term has come to mean any intense late phase of design, or even an independent intense design effort. The Department of Architecture at Washington currently schedules a charrette, a week-long study of a particular design problem, at the beginning of spring term.

6. For Pries see Drew Rocker in Jeffrey Karl Ochsner, *Shaping Seattle Architecture* (Seattle: University of Washington Press, 1994), pp. 228-33. At the time of writing Ochsner had in preparation a detailed biography of Pries, and he kindly shared the manuscript, in draft, with us.

7. Carl Frelinghuysen Gould was the designing partner in the firm of Bebb and Gould, who had prepared Washington's brilliant campus master plan in 1914, and by 1923 had completed several campus buildings. The most important of them, Suzzallo Library, was in construction in 1923. See T. William Booth and William H. Wilson, *Carl F. Gould: A Life in Architecture and the Arts* (Seattle: University of Washington Press, 1995).

8. Pries's own house of 1948-50 illustrates his remarkable eclecticism. The entry was reached by ascending a winding flight of concrete steps edged by concrete block bastions and antique Japanese stone lanterns. At the top, framed by walls of concrete block, was the front door, made from a Balinese bedstead. At either side were Native American motifs; the number plate above was verdigris copper with Vitruvian numerals. Inside, a stair led up to the living room, which looked east to a gracious back garden seen through industrial sash. On one wall was a Nolli map of Rome; the ceiling was of cork, painted to replicate Navaho sand paintings; the soffit of the deep roof overhang beyond the industrial sash was also painted with Native American motifs. Dining room walls, including the door to the kitchen, were lined with books; shoji screens could mask, or reveal, the industrial-sash corner window. At door-head height around the dining room a frieze presented, in a Wrightian typeface, a quotation from Ruskin. Pries invited students to the house often; it was to some significant degree a school annex. Most students saw it as an extension of his teaching, and there is reason to think that he meant them to do so. Pries died in 1968; his house is now much remodeled.

9. Interview, Lovett/Booth, October 2000.

10. The curriculum for the Bachelor of Architecture degree, from the early twentieth century until its widespread replacement by alternate curricula in the 1970s, entailed five years—typically five intense years—of study.

For a few years after 1944, however, the curriculum was compressed into four even more intense years, to accommodate the returning serviceman's urgent need to begin a career delayed by the war.

11. And I. M. Pei's later Hancock Building opposite H. H. Richardson's Trinity Church.

12. Interview Lovett/Booth, October 2000.

13. Ibid..

14. See Gilbert Herbert, *The Dream of the Factory-Built House: Walter Gropius and Conrad Wachsmann* (Cambridge, Mass.: MIT Press, 1984).

15. On *Domus*, see Brian McLaren, "Continuity and Discontinuity," *Column 5* (the journal of architecture, University of Washington) 16: 28-31.

16. He was also invited at this time to join Eero Saarinen's office in Birmingham, Michigan. But just having returned to Seattle from Cambridge, he and Eileen felt the time was not right for another uprooting.

17. Lovett was the twenty-second member of the community, of an eventual forty. Other Hilltop residents included architect Perry Johanson, marine biologist Victor Scheffer, and historians Stull Holt and Charles Gates.

18. The conoidal brick fireplace in this house and that in the one immediately to follow, for Lovett's parents, were, according to Lovett, a "homage to Aalto."

19. The list includes Eero Saarinen, Paul Rudolph, Edward Stone, Skidmore, Owings, and Merrill, Paul Hayden Kirk, Louis I. Kahn, and Philip Johnson, all of whom later found different modes; and Mies himself, who didn't.

20. Albert Frey, *In Search of a Living Architecture* (New York: Architectural Book Publishing Co., 1949).

21. Interview Lovett/Booth, October 2000.

22. Frey, *In Search*, p. 29.

23. Ibid.

24. Ibid., p. 50.

25. Personal communication, Lovett to Booth/Hildebrand, 21 December 2000.

26. The house was published in *Interiors* 112 (June 1953):100-105; *Arts and Architecture* 70 (July 1953):28-29; *L'Architecture d'Aujourd'hui* (Paris) 52 (February 1954):10-11; and *Informes de la Construction* (Madrid) 90 (April 1957).

27. This was the period in which Mies had long since seen several items to production, Eero Saarinen was designing the Womb Chair and the Pedestal series, Harry Bertoia was involved with his wire mesh chairs, and Charles and Ray Eames were working out several pieces including the much-copied Eames Lounge Chair of 1956, of plywood, aluminum, and leather. Many of these designs are still in production and for decades have been regarded as classics. And Aalto's plywood and bentwood furniture was widely known. All of these designs were intended to be machine-made and mass-produced, although Mies's designs in particular involved a lot of highly skilled handwork, and thus were very expensive indeed. The Eames Lounge Chair, still in production, is expensive because of fine materials—choice leather and flawless rosewood plywood—but is entirely mass-producible.

28. Interview, Lovett/Booth, October 2000.

29. Ibid.

30. In 1963 Gutbrod taught at Washington as its first Walker-Ames Professor of Architecture.

31. The Exposition's best-known structure now is certainly the Space Needle, designed by John Graham Jr. and Lovett's University faculty colleague Victor Steinbrueck. Steinbrueck would later be famous for his key role in preserving Seattle's Pike Place Market, in which Arne Bystrom was also closely involved. The Exposition's Coliseum Building (now drastically altered internally), an equally sophisticated design, was by Paul Thiry, Bystrom's first architectural employer.

32. Lovett cites, as few observers have done, the "cave" in the well-known Charles and Ray Eames house in Pacific Palisades, California, of 1945-49, as a parallel example.

While Lovett derived these characteristics intuitively, they can now be cognitively argued as having a widespread intuitive human appeal. The grove or cave is the necessary place of protection from climate and predator; it looks to and opens to the meadow, the place of foraging and hunting. From the grove or cave one can assess the meadow for resources and dangers; from the meadow one can see and, as necessary, retreat to the refuge. Our distant ancestors who were intuitively drawn to this juxtaposition of spaces improved their chances of living to produce offspring, and of bringing those offspring to adulthood to produce another such generation. As their distant genetic heirs, we seem to possess the same attraction to such spaces. For research and publication of this theory see Jay Appelton, *The Experience of Landscape* (London: Wiley, 1995), and many articles and reports by Stephen and Rachel Kaplan, Gordon Orians, and Judith Heerwagen. See also Grant Hildebrand, *The Wright Space* (Seattle: University of Washington Press, 1991), and *Origins of Architectural Pleasure* (Berkeley: University of California Press, 1999).

33. In Lovett's case there are two documented connections. First, Lovett, with Gene Zema and Daniel Streissguth, was architect for the University's Nuclear Reactor Building, designed in 1960 when Yamasaki headed the Design Committee; Lovett remembers some abrasive meetings with that committee. Second, Lovett and Kahn were invited participants at the 1959 CIAM conference at Otterlo, a conference that also included Aldo Van Eyck.

Chapter 3: The Crane Island Retreat

1. Larry Woodin, "Wendell Lovett, Architect" (Master's thesis, Department of Architecture, University of Washington, 1979), p. 135.

2. Stark Young, *Selected Poems of Sidney Lanier* (New York: Scribners, 1947): "The Marshes of Glynn," line 37.

3. Stephen and Rachel Kaplan, "Aesthetics, Affect, and Cognition: Environmental Preference from an Evolutionary Perspective," *Environment and Behavior* 19:1 (January 1987): 3.

4. In 1966, and first used in his house for Jack and Donna Melill on Mercer Island, in 1968. Although the Toetoaster, like its predecessor the Firehood, is made of sheet metal in singly curved surfaces, and is therefore a logical design for mass production, the disposition of the axes and the shapes of the edges present a more complex, almost voluptuous, geometry. The Toetoaster remains a remarkably handsome sculptural form. But the original Firehood had created an industry, and Lovett's new design was no longer the only thing of its kind. It did not have an equal market success.

5. Lanier, "Marshes," lines 36, 38.

Chapter 4: Lovett's Mature Career

1. Quoted in Larry Woodin, "Wendell Lovett, Architect" (Master's thesis, Department of Architecture, University of Washington, 1979), p. 151.

2. This spatial organization is in many respects similar to that repeatedly used by Frank Lloyd Wright in his houses dating from about 1902 to 1952, but the similarity is entirely coincidental, because Lovett has never regarded Wright as an exemplar. Furthermore, in bringing the stairway out into the living space at the midpoint of its descent, Lovett includes a spatial experience that has no equivalent in Wright's work.

3. Williams admires both sides of Wendell's career, and is himself interested in teaching.

4. From a typed description for awards-submission purposes, undated, in the Lovett office files.

5. Ibid.

6. From a videotaped interview, Lovett to Booth, at the Cutler-Girdler house in October 1999.

7. These are clearly diagrammed in Juhani Pallasmaa, *Alvar Aalto: The Villa Mairea*, (Helsinki: Alvar Aalto Foundation, 1998), p. 81.

8. From a videotaped interview (see note 6 above).

9. Interview, Lovett/Booth, October 2000.

10. The award "recognizes distinguished lifetime achievement in architecture, including design and professional practice, and service to the profession, the community, and the arts, or any combination of these." The medal was first awarded in 1984 to Paul Thiry and Paul Hayden Kirk.

Chapter 5: Arne Bystrom's Formative Years

1. The preceding information and this quoted comment are from various interviews, Bystrom/Booth-Hildebrand, during the spring of 2002.

2. Interview, Bystrom/Hildebrand, April 2003.

3. Other faculty of the time remember occasions of intense and severe differences between contending factions. None were more intense and severe, apparently, than those between Pries and Lovett.

4. As quoted in Are Risto Oyasaeter, "The Role of Wood, Craftsmanship and Detail in the Residential Work of Arne Bystrom" (Master's thesis, Department of Architecture, University of Washington, 1997), p. 7.

5. One of the more memorable comments is Philip Johnson's famous quip of the 1950s that Wright was "the greatest American architect of the nineteenth century." It must be added, however, that Johnson later handsomely retracted his quip, acknowledging that, to develop his own direction at the time, he, like so many others, had to find some way to get past Wright's titanic presence. There were also dramatic exceptions to the ostracism. Mies himself, in the 1950s, honored Wright in a memorably eloquent metaphor, likening him to "a great tree in a vast meadow, that with every passing year attains a more noble crown." Booth, at Harvard GSD at the time of Wright's death in April 1959, remembers Professor Edward Sekler's extemporaneous,

heartfelt, and moving eulogy.

6. From typed notes for a talk about the Raft River retreat and the Dennis house, undated, in the Bystrom office files.

7. Banister Fletcher, *A History of Architecture on the Comparative Method, for students, craftsmen, & amateurs* (London: Batsford, 1st ed., 1896). When Bystrom was in school the perennial classic would have been in its fourteenth edition, of 1948, and its fifteenth, of 1950, and its author had become Sir Banister Fletcher, Knt.

8. We are indebted to Jeffrey Karl Ochsner for sharing with us his authoritative pending manuscript on Pries, from which we have drawn much information.

9. Interview, Lien/Booth, February 2003.

10. Henry Adams's *Mont-Saint-Michel and Chartres* was privately printed in 1904, and first publicly issued in 1913, with energetic encouragement from Ralph Adams Cram (no relation) and support from the American Institute of Architects. In Bystrom's years, and for a long time thereafter, it was a staple text in many architecture schools including Washington, and was often awarded as a prize for some achievement. Now a classic, it is rarely out of print; some recent editions are handsomely illustrated in color. Although some of Adams's facts and interpretations must yield to more recent knowledge, the book is still richly rewarding.

11. Thiry is often cited as simply "the earliest" Seattle modernist. But Jeffrey Ochsner has found a photo, dated "1932," that puts the issue in some doubt. It portrays a striking residential example of European modernism, built in the Washington Park neighborhood, though without a street address. The architect is unknown, and the house itself either no longer exists or has been remodeled beyond recognition. If by a Seattle architect, his claim would predate Thiry's by at least three years. For a brief account of Thiry's life and career see Meredith Clausen's essay in Jeffrey Karl Ochsner, ed., *Shaping Seattle*

Architecture (Seattle: University of Washington Press, 1994, rev. 1998), pp. 246-51.

12. Oyasaeter, "The Role of Wood," p. 8.

13. Personal comment to Hildebrand, March 2002.

14. For a more detailed discussion of Kirk, see David A. Rash's essay in Ochsner, *Shaping*, pp. 252-57.

15. Such logs—"peeler logs"—were typically available as inexpensive byproducts of plywood manufacture. They were the remaining cores of logs originally of much larger diameter which, at a certain point, could no longer be effectively turned against the veneer knives.

Chapter 6: The Raft River Retreat

1. See Chapter 2, above, note 17.

2. From typed notes for a talk, undated, in the Bystrom office files.

3. Robert Venturi, *Complexity and Contradiction in Architecture* (New York: Museum of Modern Art, 1966). See also Prologue, above, note 2.

Chapter 7: Bystrom's Mature Career

1. Are Risto Oyasaeter, "The Role of Wood, Craftsmanship and Detail in the Residential Work of Arne Bystrom" (Master's thesis, Department of Architecture, University of Washington, 1997), p. 54.

2. From typed notes for awards-submission material, undated, in the Bystrom office files.

3. The Moore exterior equally suggests several masterpieces of the Shingle Style, notably McKim, Mead and White's mountainously gabled William Low House in Bristol, Rhode Island, of 1883.

4. From typed notes for a talk, undated, in the Bystrom office files.

5. The phrase is borrowed from Australian architect Glenn Murcutt, who often uses it to describe one of the ways in which he believes his remarkable projects can respect the ecology of the Australian outback.

6. Typed notes for award-submission material, undated, in the Bystrom office files.

7. Duo Dickenson, *Small Houses for the Next Century* (Quebec: Kingsport Press, 1986), pp. 61-62.

8. Oyasaeter's words, cited in "The Role of Wood," p. 40.

9. Typed notes for award-submission material, undated, in the Bystrom office files.

Chapter 8: The Villa Simonyi

1. For anyone versed in the story of twentieth-century architecture the word "villa" will immediately bring to mind two classics: Le Corbusier's Villa Savoye of 1929, and Aalto's Villa Mairea of 1937-39. Aalto's role in Lovett's thoughts has been discussed herein at length, and it will be remembered that Corbu was the hero of Lovett's college years. In addition, Simonyi's emphasis on the elevator, and his reference to a "Moonbase," suggest Corbu's famous aphorism "a house is a machine for living," while the Euclidian geometry of elements such as the cylindrical duct housings in the small original gallery reprises Corbu's definition of architecture as "the correct and magnificent play of forms in the sun."

2. Typed memo on the project, undated, in the Lovett office files.

3. The term might be considered a reasonable encapsulation of a long-standing definition of the aesthetic experience—generally regarded—as necessarily involving order, structure, or coherence, complemented by variety, surprise, or permutation. The earliest example of which we are aware is William Wordsworth's observation, in "Preface to *Lyrical Ballads*," that poetry depends upon "similitude in dissimilitude"; his point is rephrased in the next century by Gerard Manley Hopkins as "likeness tempered with difference." There has been a lot of more recent literature on the subject, from commentators in many fields, representing both theoretical and empirical work; one of the most articulate

discussions is Nicholas Humphrey, "Natural Aesthetics," in Byron Mikellides, ed., *Architecture for People* (London: Studio Vista, 1980), from which the above quotation from Hopkins is taken (p. 65).

Chapter 9: The Dennis House

1. Bystrom, typed notes on the Dennis house, undated, Bystrom office files.

2. This approach also has precedent in Wright; the exploitation of the eave "margin" at the Edwin Cheney house in Oak Park of 1904 is one example among many.

3. We noted in Chapter 7 that the Dennis house is the largest and the most elaborate of the stave-church family. It is also obviously atypical in that while its structure and skin are autonomous, the skin does not enclose and therefore protect the structure. This may be regrettable on theoretical grounds, but given the program of the house, and its consequent size, a minimalist planar cladding would have been impossibly scaleless and monumental.

4. Bystrom, typed notes (see note 1 above).

5. Ibid. At another location in these notes Bystrom refers to the struts as "historically similar to . . . Aalto." The similarity, presumably, would be to the Council Chamber ceiling struts of the Saynatsalo Town Hall. The brackets reiterate, in a simpler, more Euclidean geometry, those of innumerable Chinese religious and governmental structures, and innumerable Japanese temples deriving from Chinese influence. Of Chinese examples, the various buildings of the Forbidden City are the best known; of Japanese, perhaps the Buddhist complex of Horiyu-ji at Nara, and the Tokugawa shrine at Nikko. The origins of bracing struts in wooden structures go back into the depths of time.

6. The supposedly modernist mandate for structural honesty, or honesty of structural expression, is obviously violated here. But in our synopses of modernism we have not emphasized that mandate, because it is also violated in a plethora of modernist examples of every stripe. Hugh Morrison noted, sixty-five years ago, that Louis Sullivan's Wainwright and Guaranty buildings include actual bearing columns only in every other pier above the second floor, while the more lightly loaded corner pier in both buildings is uniquely large in finished dimension. Sullivan's Carson Pirie Scott store has always presented the puzzle of the wonderful but bizarre ornament that commands the lower two floors. The actual structure of Aalto's Villa Mairea is at some places blatantly evident to the eye, and elsewhere not evident at all. The columns of Mies's Farnsworth house are welded to the sides of the bearing fascia, which in terms of the structural relationship of column to beam is absurd. The structure of Le Corbusier's Ronchamp is in no way visibly expressed, and is, in some respects, the opposite of what the eye would have us infer. And of course there are innumerable premodern historical examples, from the attached half-columns of the Colosseum to the redundant end-span suspenders of Thomas Telford's Menai Straits Bridge. Whether Bystrom's columnar sleight-of-hand can equally claim our suspension of disbelief is, of course, a judgment call.

7. Oyasaeter, "The Role of Wood," p. 67.

8. Bystrom, typed notes (see n. 1).

9. Wayne N. T. Fujii, ed., *GA Houses 21* (Tokyo: Edita, 1987), p. 64.

10. Bystrom, typed notes (see note 1 above).

11. Sigfried Giedion, *Space, Time, and Architecture: The Growth of a New Tradition* (Cambridge: Harvard University Press, 1967 [1st ed. 1941]), pp. 480-82.

Index

Aalto, Alvar, 4, 9, 12–14, 15, 22, 155n18, 155n27,
    159nn5–6; and Baker House Residence Hall
    (MIT), 12, 13–14; and Dennis house, 124; and
    Imatra church, 24–25, 45; influence on Lovett,
    12–14, 19, 20, 22–23, 24–25, 45, 46, 129, 130;
    and Mount Angel Seminary library, 25; and
    Otaniemi Technical University lecture hall, 25,
    45; and Viipuri library, 20; and Villa Mairea, 13,
    45, 46, 159n6
Adams, Henry, 54, 157n10
AIA Seattle: Medal, 48, 87, 157n10
American Institute of Architects (AIA), 12, 37, 52,
    53, 68, 109
Anderson, Stuart, 57, 59, 130, 153n3
Anthropomorphism, 17, 19, 20, 34–36, 37, 92, 100,
    104
Art Nouveau, 119

Bain, William, 11
Bassetti, Fred, 14–15, 17, 130
Bassetti and Morse, 14, 16
Bauhaus, 4, 10–11, 52, 129
Bellevue, Washington, 59. See also Hilltop commu-
    nity
"Bikini" chair (Lovett), 16, 17
"Black Angus" restaurants (Bystrom), 59–60, 71,
    72, 76, 130, 153n3
Boeing Company, 9, 51
Bower, Ted, 19
Breuer, Marcel, 3, 11
Bystrom, Albin, 51, 57
Bystrom, Arne. See Bystrom, Carl Arne
Bystrom, Ashley, 57
Bystrom, Carl, 57
Bystrom, Carl Arne, 4, 6–7, 51, 57, 130–31; and
    Bauhaus, 52, 55, 129; and Connelly-Pailthorp
    cabin, 82, 85; and Dennis house, 109, 113, 124;
    elected Fellow of AIA, 76–77; European tour
    of, 53–54, 130; and Kempton cabin, 78;
    Lovett's influence on, 52, 56, 58; and Moore

house, 71, 73, 75; and Pike Place Market, 70–
    71, 155n31; and Raft River retreat, 63, 64, 65–
    66; receives AIA Seattle Medal, 87; at Univer-
    sity of Washington, 51–53; Wright's influence
    on, 52–53, 55, 129, 130
Bystrom, Martha Hammerose, 51
Bystrom, Valerie Broze, 57
Bystrom (Albin) house (Bystrom), 57
Bystrom offices (Bystrom), 57–58, 71

Calatrava, Santiago, 100, 130
Cascade Mountains, 37
"Cave" and "meadow," 155–56n32; and Crane
    Island retreat (Lovett), 28–31; and Cutler-
    Girdler house (Lovett), 44–45, 47; and Dennis
    house (Bystrom), 122, 123–24; and Hilltop
    remodeling (Lovett), 22; and Morrison-Weston
    house (Lovett), 37, 39; and Scofield house
    (Lovett), 34–36; and Villa Simonyi (Lovett), 98,
    104
Century Building (Bystrom and Greco), 58–59
Century 21 "umbrellas," 20
Complexity and Contradiction in Architecture (Venturi),
    24, 67, 153n2
Connelly-Pailthorp cabin (Bystrom), 82–86
Covarrubias, Miguel, 11
Covarrubias, Susana, 41
Crane Island retreat (Lovett), 2, 4–5, 26–31, 65
Cret, Paul P., 11
Cutler-Girdler house (Lovett), 39–49, 104

Deception, Mount, 51. See also Olympic Moun-
    tains
Dennis house (Bystrom), 5–6, 77, 108–27
Details, informing role of: 3, 6–7; in Century 21
    "umbrellas" (Lovett), 19; in Connelly-Pailthorp
    cabin (Bystrom), 84–85; in Crane Island retreat
    (Lovett), 27–28; in Cutler-Girdler house
    (Lovett), 44, 48; in Dennis house (Bystrom),
    114–15, 116–20, 122–23, 125–26; in furniture
    design, 16, 91; in Hilltop remodeling (Lovett),
    20–21; in Kempton cabin (Bystrom), 81; in Lien
    house (Bystrom), 56–57; in Moore house
    (Bystrom), 73; in Raft River retreat (Bystrom),
    65–66; in Villa Simonyi (Lovett), 91, 93–94, 96–
    97, 100–102, 103; in work of Greene and

Greene, 125–26
Dickenson, Duo, 81–82
Domus, 14, 15, 16, 19, 24, 36, 98, 129

Eade, Gilbert, 130
Eames, Charles and Ray, 155n27, 155n32
École des Beaux-Arts, 8, 9–10, 52, 54, 131, 154n3
Erskine, Ralph, 4, 19, 24, 36, 98

"Firehood" fireplace (Lovett), 15, 16, 17, 54
Frey, Albert, 15

Gaudi, Antonio, 153n1
Gehry, Frank, 45, 104
Gidion, Siegfried, 124
Gould, Carl F., 11, 154n7
Greco, James, 55–59
Greene, Charles and Henry. *See* Greene and Greene
Greene and Greene, 4, 7, 114, 124, 125–26, 130
Gropius, Walter, 11, 14, 15, 129, 153n1
Gutbrod, Rolf, 4, 18–19, 36, 155n30

Harvard Graduate School of Design, 12, 14–15, 129
Hilltop community (Bellevue, WA), 15, 17

Johnson, Philip, 155n19, 157n5
Jung, Carl, 28–30, 130

Kahn, Albert, 153n1
Kahn, Louis I., 23–24, 59, 155n19, 156n33
Kaplan, Stephen and Rachel, 30, 155–56n32, 156n3
Kempton cabin (Bystrom), 77–82, 110
Kirk, Paul Hayden, 23, 55, 56–57, 58, 67, 154n3, 155n19, 157n10

Lanier, Sidney ("The Marshes of Glynn"), 30–31
Larsen house (Lovett), 37, 39
Le Corbusier, 3, 4, 11, 12, 13, 15, 23, 52, 129, 153n1, 158n1
Leger, Fernand (*La Partie de la Campagne*), 96
Leonhardt, Fritz, 19, 100
Lichtenstein, Roy, 6, 89
Liebeskind, Daniel, 45, 104
Lien, Carsten, 51, 53
Lien house (Bystrom), 55–57
Lovett, Clare, 19
Lovett, Corrie, 10
Lovett, Eileen Whitson, 12
Lovett, Pearl Harper, 9

Lovett, Wallace, 9
Lovett, Wendell Harper, 4, 6–7, 9, 12, 17, 130–31; Aalto's influence, 12–14, 20, 22–23, 24–25; and anthropomorphism, 17, 19, 34–36, 37, 92, 100, 104; at Bassetti and Morse, 14; and Dennis house, 122, 123–24; elected Fellow of AIA, 37; and industrial design, 15, 16, 17, 31, 54, 91; influence on Bystrom, 52, 56, 58; and mechanistic detail, 7, 9, 14, 15, 16, 17, 19, 20–21, 27–28, 36, 44, 48, 94, 96, 97, 101–2; at MIT, 12–14; and music, 9, 19, 47, 105; receives AIA Seattle Medal, 48; revised beliefs of, 17–18, 22–23; as teacher, 41, 52; at Technical Institute of Stuttgart, 18–19; at University of Washington, 9–13
Lovett (Wallace) house (Lovett), 16–17
Lovett (Wendell) house (Lovett): original, 15–16; remodeling, 20–23, 25, 65, 97, 130

Mackinlay, Ian, 109
Maillart, Robert, 12, 24, 100, 130
"Marshes of Glynn, The," (Lanier), 30–31
Massachusetts Institute of Technology (MIT), 12–14, 15, 17, 52, 129, 130
McKim, Mead, and White, 158n3
Medina, Washington: Cutler-Girdler house (Lovett), 34–39; Villa Simonyi (Lovett), 5–6, 88–107
Mendelssohn, Erich, 153n1
Mercer Island, Washington, 34–36, 45
Mies van der Rohe, Ludwig, 3, 11, 15, 52, 55–57, 59, 155n19, 155n27, 157n5; and ornament, 3, 159n6
Miller house (Lovett), 33–34
MIT. *See* Massachusetts Institute of Technology
Modernism: 3–4, 7, 10, 11, 12, 13, 67; challenges to, 4, 23–24; enrichment of, 6, 131; historical background of, 3; technological emphasis of, 3–4, 14, 15–16, 19, 28; tenets of, 3, 6, 64–65, 104–5, 129, 130; ubiquity of, 14, 15, 23, 56
Moore, Charles, 24, 153n2
Moore house (Bystrom), 71, 73–77, 110
Morrison-Weston house (Lovett), 37–41
Mumford, Lewis, 4, 153n1
Murcutt, Glenn, 153n2, 158n5

Naramore, Bain, Brady and Johanson, 14

Obstruction Island, 77–82
Ochsner, Jeffrey Karl, 154n4, 157n6
Olympic Mountains, 51, 71, 76

Partie de la Campagne, La (Leger), 96
Pei, I. M., 153n2, 155n11
Postmodernism, 24, 67, 131, 153n2
Pries, Lionel Henry "Spike," 11–12, 52, 53, 56, 129, 154n6, 154n8, 157n8
Priteca, Marcus, 9

Raft River retreat (Bystrom), 4, 5, 62–68, 82, 85, 109
Rainier, Mount, 37
Ransome, Ernest, 153n1
Rapson, Ralph, 13
Reed house (Lovett), 17, 18, 100
Rogers, Ernesto, 15
Rudolph, Paul, 23, 58–59, 155n19

Saarinen, Eero, 23, 56, 129, 155n19, 155n27
Saarinen, Eliel, 4, 129; and Cranbrook, 9
Scarpa, Carlo, 15, 24, 90, 93
Scofield house (Lovett), 34–37, 98
Seattle, Washington, 4, 6, 7, 9, 11, 14; Ballard neighborhood, 51; bathhouses (Bystrom), 59–60, 130; "Black Angus" restaurants (Bystrom), 59; Bystrom offices (Bystrom), 57, 70–71; Century Building (Bystrom), 58; Century 21 exposition, 19, 20; Larsen house (Lovett), 37; Morrison-Weston house (Lovett), 37; Pike Place Market, 71, 155n31
Seattle bathhouses (Bystrom), 59–60, 130
Seckler, Edward, 157n5
Simonyi, Charles, 89–90
Simonyi house. *See* Villa Simonyi
Sodergren, Evert, 71, 119
Stave church: and Dennis house (Bystrom), 77, 159n3; examples, 71–72, 84; as influence on Bystrom, 71–72, 73–75, 77, 79, 114, 124, 130
Steinbrueck, Victor, 155n31
Stern, Robert A. M., 153n2
"Stop" and "go" spaces, 21, 37, 44, 51, 95, 98, 123–24
"Street" (as interior circulation), 38, 44, 95–96
Streissguth, Daniel, 156n33
Structure, informing role of: 3, 7, 12, 15, 19, 56–57, 130; in "Black Angus" restaurants (Bystrom), 59; in Connelly-Pailthorp cabin (Bystrom), 85; in Crane Island retreat (Lovett), 27–28; in Dennis house (Bystrom), 113–14; in Kempton cabin (Bystrom), 79–81; in Moore house (Bystrom), 73–75; in Norwegian stave-church, 71–72; in Raft River retreat (Bystrom), 65–67; in Villa Simonyi (Lovett), 100–102

Stuttgart. *See* Technical Institute of Stuttgart
Sullivan, Louis, 3, 4, 153n1, 159n6
Sun Valley, Idaho, 5, 108–27 *passim*

Technical Institute of Stuttgart 18–19, 20, 22, 130
Telford, Thomas, 3, 159n6
Terry, Roland, 154n3
Thiry, Paul, 54, 130, 155n31, 157n11
"Toetoaster" fireplace (Lovett), 31, 156n4

University of Washington, 9, 11–12, 15, 18, 39–41, 51–53, 129, 154–55n10

Vasarely, Victor, 6, 89, 90, 92, 94
Venturi, Robert (*Complexity and Contradiction in Architecture*), 24, 67, 153n2
Villa Simonyi (Lovett), 5–6, 7, 39, 41, 88–107

Wachsmann, Conrad, 15
Washington, Lake, 37, 43, 45
Whidbey Island, Washington: Connelly-Pailthorp cabin (Bystrom), 82–87; Miller house (Lovett), 33–34; Moore house (Bystrom), 71, 73–76
Whittaker, James, 63
Willcox, W. R. B., 9
Williams, Charles J., III, 39–41, 45–46, 156n3
Wright, Frank Lloyd, 3, 4, 9, 15, 52–53, 55, 59, 110, 124, 129, 130, 153n1, 156n2, 157n5, 159n2

Yamasaki, Minoru, 23, 156n33

Zarina, Astra, 23
Zech house (Bystrom), 57
Zema, Gene, 156n33